Freedom in Laughter

SUNY series in African American Studies

John R. Howard and Robert C. Smith, editors

Freedom in Laughter

*Dick Gregory, Bill Cosby,
and the Civil Rights Movement*

MALCOLM FRIERSON

Published by State University of New York Press, Albany

© 2020 State University of New York

All rights reserved

No part of this book may be used or reproduced in any manner whatsoever without written permission. No part of this book may be stored in a retrieval system or transmitted in any form or by any means including electronic, electrostatic, magnetic tape, mechanical, photocopying, recording, or otherwise without the prior permission in writing of the publisher.

For information, contact State University of New York Press, Albany, NY
www.sunypress.edu

Library of Congress Cataloging-in-Publication Data

Names: Frierson, Malcolm, 1974– author.
Title: Freedom in laughter : Dick Gregory, Bill Cosby, and the civil rights movement / Malcolm Frierson.
Description: Albany : State University of New York Press, 2020. | Series: SUNY series in african american studies | Includes bibliographical references and index.
Identifiers: LCCN 2019036169 | ISBN 9781438479071 (hardcover : alk. paper) | ISBN 9781438479064 (pbk. : alk. paper) | ISBN 9781438479088 (ebook)
Subjects: LCSH: Gregory, Dick. | Cosby, Bill, 1937– | African Americans—Civil rights. | African American entertainers—Biography. | Civil rights workers—United States—Biography. | Comedians—United States—Biography. | African Americans—Segregation—Humor.
Classification: LCC E185.61 .F895 2020 | DDC 323.1196/073—dc23
LC record available at https://lccn.loc.gov/2019036169

10 9 8 7 6 5 4 3 2 1

For Nicole

Contents

List of Illustrations	ix
Acknowledgments	xi
Introduction: Humor Matters	xv
Chapter 1 The Green Room	1
Chapter 2 Coming to the Stage	21
Chapter 3 All of the Lights	41

photo gallery following page 68

Chapter 4 Black Comedy, Black Power	69
Chapter 5 Edutainment	89
Epilogue	113
Notes	131
Works Cited	153
Index	159

Illustrations

The photos appear as a gallery after page 68

Figure 1.1   Dick Gregory at Southern Illinois University

Figure 1.2   Bill Cosby at Temple University

Figure 2.1   Dick Gregory and Mike Douglas

Figure 2.2   Bill Cosby performing stand-up

Figure 3.1   Dick Gregory and Ossie Davis

Figure 3.2   Bill Cosby and Sidney Poitier

Acknowledgments

This book began the moment that my college roommates dared me to enter a campus talent competition. Not only did I accept, but I won first place with an original stand-up comedy routine. Within two years, I became a professional comedian with a budding career, big-time agent, and invitation to take my talents to Los Angeles. I balked. My fear was that the label of "comedian" would ruin my goal to become a scholar and activist. *Who would take me seriously?* I asked myself. So, rather than trying to make it as a Martin Lawrence with political interests, I instead chose to become an academic with an interest in humor. I wish I knew then what I know now! Nonetheless, many thanks to my college roomies, Ralph Johnson and Anthony K., for your initial challenge, and to Arnez J and Nephew Tommy for taking a "newjack" under your wing.

The University of Memphis Department of History provided the research and travel funding to complete this study. Janann Sherman, this book, as well as our wonderful friendship, found its shape in your Dissertation Support Group meetings. Thank you for being in my corner when I needed you most. Karen Bradley, your kindness, professionalism, and genuine conversations made working with you enjoyable. Beverly Bond, Charles Crawford, and Ed Yancey, thank you for investing in this project. Aram Goudsouzian, words cannot do justice to the support you gave at every stage in this process. From conceptualization to publication, this book reflects a conversation that you and I began several years ago. I could not have made a better choice for an advisor to guide that discussion.

The New York Library for the Performing Arts and Schomburg Center for Research in Black Culture shared archival resources toward the publication of this work. Heartfelt thanks to those who fielded document requests and worked diligently to assist my research. The Special Collections Research Center, Southern Illinois University Carbondale Library and the Charles L. Blockson Afro-American Collection, Temple University Libraries provided images that appear in this book. Special thanks to both institutions for speedy turnaround times. Michael Rinella, my editor at SUNY Press, thank you for your exceptional diligence and support.

Edmund Abaka and Nupur Chaudhuri, you've helped me remain steady through some turbulent stretches since I began my journey in academia. This book, in a very real sense, is evidence of your mentorship and larger work. Audrey McCluskey, thank you for taking the time to assist my transition from doctoral candidate to colleague. Ameenah Shakir, your friendship has been a gift for fifteen years and counting. You nurture my intellect, give the best advice, and crack me up effortlessly through the good and bad. I *see* you! Monique Bedasse, John Gustavsen, Cecile Houry, Jack Lorenzini, and Chanelle Rose, thank you for your feedback and friendship over the years.

Lane College offered my first full-time faculty position. I felt the HBCU love from my first day to my last. I'm indebted to Carleen Jackson and Linda Theus, especially, for fully orienting me to higher education while encouraging me not to lose sight of this project.

My tenure at North Lake College connected me to an incredible group of professionals who made me feel "home." Christa Slejko, the opportunity to share the final stages of this research with the NLC campus community will always be a highlight of my career. Roy Vu, your support of my academic as well as creative endeavors is truly appreciated. Tish Waters Hearne, I look forward to discussing the arguments in this book endlessly. There are so many more special people in my North Lake College family than I have room to mention. Please forgive the omissions. Lastly, and quite personally, I want to acknowledge my NLC colleagues who helped lift me during unfortunate life events prior to this book's completion. James Duran, Phyllis Elmore, Shawnda Floyd, Daryl Howard, Arthur James, Shani Suber, Roy Vu—again, more names than I have room to mention—thank you for caring and seeing me through.

My mom, Muriel Frierson, gave me the spirit of ambition. My dad, Earnest Frierson, gave me direction. This book honors you both. Marcus, Susan, and Mario, my siblings, thank you for understanding and validating my lifelong idiosyncrasies with love. This book is all of ours.

Nicole, my darling wife, you coauthored this book through your consistently tender love that strengthens me more than you know. We've come so far, and I've learned so much about partnership along the way. Thank you for understanding my writing process and tolerating the organized mess of books and papers when I kick into high gear. Thank you for sitting and thinking with me every time I asked for five minutes to get your thoughts about my ideas (even though you knew it would take so much longer). Thank you for placing your career on hold to navigate our family through a storm. And thank you for making me Eva's dad. This is my best life, "on the ocean," just like we planned. I love you, I love you, I love you.

Introduction

Humor Matters

In the 1960s, Dick Gregory and Bill Cosby electrified white audiences with comedy acts that echoed millions of African American voices demanding political, social, and economic equality. Gregory led the paradigm shift with an edgy brand of racial humor that represented African Americans seeking immediate gains. He shocked whites with his biting satire and transformed the comic stage into a platform for protest and leadership in the African American struggle for freedom. Cosby, a slightly younger comedian, soon followed with a less jarring style that featured family-friendly storytelling and excluded racial material. He patiently and strategically allowed the appeal of humor rooted in universal humanity to nudge whites toward viewing African Americans as equals. Gregory and Cosby fused art and politics to a degree comparable to more recognized cultural celebrities, such as Muhammad Ali, Harry Belafonte, and Sammy Davis Jr. Both comedians contributed to the advancement of civil and human rights in America. Their careers transcended the boundaries in which humorists are often confined.

Humor is a universal language that consists of simple as well as deeply perceptive observations of lifeways, such as music, dress, government, and child rearing, that exist within a specific culture. It unifies groups and societies by communicating members' thoughts regarding established norms, quite often coupling them with exaggeration, oddity, or ridiculousness. Dexter Gordon asserts that "humor arises from passion and has always provided a serviceable channel for expressing human feelings." This idea is especially characteristic of the role of humor in the African American experience. "When the rage of the oppressed is spoken,"

Gordon posits, "humorous discourse may provide a vital rather than a merely convenient channel."[1] Gregory and Cosby employed humor as a "safe" medium through which their grievances against white supremacy could be registered. It invited less backlash than more aggressive channels, such as public protest. Using humor to defuse volatile topics proved invaluable to both comedians, who communicated serious messages in vastly different styles.

Stand-up comedy is the delivery of topical material from an individual humorist's perspective. For the most part, it is absent any scripts or props. It is a complex art form distinguishable from the retelling of humorous tales. Stand-up comedians are identifiable by their original routines, which differ widely in material, style, and timing. Performers invest considerable thought and practice in crafting their succession of bits that can work to entertain, unite, and educate audiences. Lawrence Mintz argues that stand-up comedy is the most "deeply significant form of humorous expression" as well as the "purest public comic communication."[2] Its boundaries are as infinite as each artist's imagination and rhetorical skill. Dave Chappelle, perhaps the leading current African American comedian to carry the torch of racial satire, goes to great lengths to protect that purity. Chappelle prohibits cell phones at his concerts to encourage the "opportunity for artists to really flex their muscles without the fear of the repercussion of the overly sensitive."[3]

In the 1960s, stand-up comedy provided a new channel through which ideas representative of African Americans' aims for freedom and equality could be expressed to mainstream America. Gregory and Cosby, the first African Americans to experience crossover success as professional stand-up comedians, emerged as pioneers in delivering topical material independent of the booking agents, club owners, and social order that had long repressed their comedic predecessors. Cosby reveres the long tradition of African American comedy that positioned his rise, particularly the "sad" case of Bert Williams, whose legendary talent proved no match against American racism in the early twentieth century. To obtain work, Williams and his contemporaries in the first half of the twentieth century accepted gigs that usually depicted African Americans as second-rate citizens and buffoons, which fell far short of the creative license that characterizes professional stand-up comedy. Cosby credits the 1950s as the decade when the bed of modern African American comedy received its flowering. Redd Foxx, LaWanda Page, Timmie Rogers, Nipsey Russell, Flip Wilson, Rodney Winfield, and many others in that era carried African

American stand-up comedy on the chitlin' circuit—a network of venues that played to African American audiences.[4] But they longed for broader appeal. Gregory and Cosby, conversely, felt no such constraint in the 1960s. As the nation's first professional African American stand-up comedians with mainstream success, they enjoyed an unprecedented combination of independence and top billing, which heightened the significance of the political messages embedded in their humor.

Gregory and Cosby joined a wide range of African American cultural activists in the post–World War II era whose craft doubled as weapons in the fight against Jim Crow. Aram Goudsouzian's biography of America's first dark-skinned leading man, *Sidney Poitier: Man, Actor, Icon*, documents the delicate manner in which Poitier effected advancement for African Americans through character portrayals that popularized "positive images of blacks." Suzanne Smith's study *Dancing in the Street: Motown and the Cultural Politics of Detroit* establishes the record company as a unique product of the Motor City with musicians who helped cement African American images and sounds in the cultural landscape of America and the world. Jules Tygiel's work on Jackie Robinson positions the athlete as the right man in the right sport to demonstrate that African Americans deserved equal opportunity within the playing field and beyond.[5] In *Stars for Freedom: Hollywood, Black Celebrities, and the Civil Rights Movement*, Emily Raymond reconstructs the activism of a group of African Americans who used their fame to help advance the movement. Raymond identifies Belafonte, Ossie Davis, Sammy Davis Jr., Ruby Dee, Gregory, and Poitier as the "Leading Six" celebrities involved in the struggle. A host of additional studies further examine the confluence of politics and African American culture. Gregory and Cosby entered the theater of civil rights alongside an established cast of cultural activists, although both commanded unprecedented roles as stand-up comedians.[6]

Freedom in Laughter expands the landscape of activism to include Gregory's and Cosby's often overlooked contributions to the African American struggle for freedom. Its inquiry into the background, character, and motivations of the cultural icons reveals complex identities that have yet to be investigated at length in connection to the movement. Its focus on the politics of African American comedy broadens our understanding of the fight for equality. It also juxtaposes the two leading African American comedians at the height of the Civil Rights Movement, demonstrating opposing strategies adopted by peer entertainers to attack segregation and Jim Crow. African American comedians were agents of cultural protest.

They possessed far greater access to large audiences of whites than more recognized African American activists, such as preachers, politicians, and business and organizational leaders. The subtle but powerful medium of humor licensed them to register ideas that would have been received with far greater controversy if delivered through other channels.

Gregory's and Cosby's linkage as activists who are better contextualized in comparison to one another locates them in the long tradition of racial uplift debates between African American leaders. Martin Delany and Frederick Douglass, Booker T. Washington and W.E.B. Du Bois, and Malcolm X and Martin Luther King Jr. preceded Gregory and Cosby in promoting divergent paths to black advancement. However, Gregory's and Cosby's opposing ideologies as leading contemporaries in the arena of comedy warrant stronger analysis. *Freedom in Laughter* documents the changes within and between the comedians' politics of humor and their larger significance to the movement.

Chapter 1 reconstructs the remarkably similar childhoods and young adult experiences of Gregory and Cosby. This narrative eliminates class as an explanation for their different styles as professional stand-up comedians and public espousal of civil rights and Black Power goals. Gregory and Cosby, growing up in St. Louis and Philadelphia, respectively, experienced near parallel backgrounds in education, athletics, employment, and the military prior to performing stand-up in the 1960s. Both shined shoes to earn money, served in the US armed forces, attended college on athletic scholarships, and discontinued undergraduate study to pursue careers in comedy. The congruency is astounding and quite illuminating with respect to the foundation of their later politics.

Chapter 2 documents the challenges and successes that met both comedians as they introduced a new cultural politics in African American comedy in the early 1960s. Civil rights victories, such as the *Brown* decision, and the emergence of respectable African American cultural celebrities, such as Jackie Robinson, Sidney Poitier, and the Motown lineup, helped engineer greater openness among white liberals to the African American experience. Rising numbers of whites—including Hugh Hefner, who gave Gregory his first mainstream gig in 1961—were enthralled by Gregory's uncensored African American humor, which helped pave the way for Cosby's mainstream debut in 1963. However, African Americans who had previously heard Gregory's jokes in private circles were critical of the originality of his act and the unprecedented attention it received in the white press. Cosby, like Gregory, received immediate acclaim from whites.

While most knew him as the next comedic star, they had no awareness of Cosby's strategic and painstaking efforts to carve an identity as the anti–Dick Gregory.

Chapter 3 focuses on the unprecedented fame, fortune, and creative license Gregory and Cosby experienced as acts with huge crossover success from 1963 to 1965. Both comedians enjoyed lucrative bookings and cemented themselves in American popular culture with guest appearances on *The Jack Paar Show* and *The Tonight Show*, two widely viewed television programs. Gregory and Cosby capitalized on book contracts that allowed further reach of their humor and life stories, but their comedy albums most captured the fascination of many thousands across the country. As new cultural celebrities, the comedians received friendly invitations as well as challenges from fellow African American celebrities and the press corps to join the front lines of the struggle for African American freedom, particularly in the South. Their responses proved to be polar opposites. Gregory canceled lucrative engagements in favor of participating in demonstrations, while Cosby humorously proclaimed himself "not bright enough to lead" and instead sent money to those on the front lines.[7] Tracing the comedians' bookings, earnings, stage material, and politics of representation during these years explains why Cosby, not Gregory, became the first African American to star in a continuing role on a television series, *I Spy*, in 1965.

Chapter 4 examines Black Power ideology from 1966 to 1968 and documents the extent to which Gregory and Cosby identified with its principles. Both agreed with the logic of African Americans using violence to defend themselves against racially motivated attacks, yet both maintained a personal commitment to nonviolence. Gregory accepted his first role in a motion picture during this period, but his entertainment career began to pale in comparison to his crusade against racism, corruption, and injustice. He used personal funds to run for mayor of Chicago, protest the war in Vietnam, publicize issues related to the Native American experience, and campaign for president of the United States. Meanwhile, Cosby's deracialized humor and public persona earned him greater earnings, acclaim, and opportunities as a comedian and actor. It also protected him from becoming like Gregory, whom he considered "broke and broken" after Gregory challenged American business, government, and society.[8] This chapter explains Gregory's and Cosby's increased divergence from 1966 to 1968 as a product of their responses to the radical politics that characterized the period.

Chapter 5 follows the comedians' professional activities from 1969 through the early 1970s. Facing debt caused by his near total removal from the comedy circuit and large donations to those fighting for African American equality, Gregory reemerged as a popular and controversial speaker on college campuses. From September 1969 to June 1970, his flight expenses incurred to fulfill speaking engagements totaled more than $30,000.[9] The amount suggests the earnings paid by universities for his visits; however, it represents only a fraction of the millions earned by Cosby for his acting, writing, producing, and directing in the television and film industry. Both comedians faced criticism for their respective politics and representations of race and masculinity. "Of course [Gregory is] an agitator," Alfred Aronowitz wrote in his column.[10] "Cosby projects the image of 'a kind of half-man who, had he lived at the time of Nat Turner, might have sold Turner down the river,'" Faith Berry charged.[11] Chapter 5 also investigates the comedians' evolving styles and goals, as Gregory shifted to delivering politically and racially charged messages to white youth on college campuses, while Cosby focused on delivering educational messages to adolescents across the races.

An epilogue considers the comedians' post-1970s career trajectories. Gregory continued to champion the struggle for black freedom and involved himself deeply in other human rights issues, such as campaigns to end war, poverty, and hunger worldwide. His patented formula for a nutrition shake earned him millions and helped fulfill his desire to contribute to progress in developing countries. But Gregory's unorthodox methods and outlandish rhetoric alienated many who otherwise would have supported his causes. Cosby earned his doctorate in education and continued a prosperous career in television and film. His 1980s sitcom, *The Cosby Show*, became one of the most successful productions in American television history. But Cosby's brand has suffered irreparable damage in recent years. He met severe criticism for his comments about African American parenting, naming, slang, and attire in a 2004 address known as the "Pound Cake Speech." His sexual assault conviction and dozens of additional allegations spanning decades have shattered his once towering legacy. Cosby's long reign as "America's favorite dad" is over, but for years he remained at the center of popular culture while Gregory stood on the periphery. Their differing presence in the conscience of the nation reflects their divergent politics of representation in the 1960s and early 1970s.

The civil rights era is most often symbolized by images of marches, boycotts, and fiery political leaders, but the artistic voice that championed the movement is a critical component of the broader effort required to combat segregation and Jim Crow. African American comedy in the 1960s and early 1970s embodied the anger, hope, fear, and expectations of nearly 12 million disfranchised citizens. Gregory and Cosby carried the banner of freedom on their behalf with unique and creative voices that dealt subtle, yet powerful, undercuts to American racism. Their talent in a changing America lifted them to heights previously unimaginable for African American stand-up comedians. The world became their stage.

Chapter 1

The Green Room

Young Dick Gregory was an easy target for ridicule. He was one of the poorest kids on his St. Louis block, and everyone knew he was without a father in his home. He initially responded to insults by running home and crying, but in time figured out that humor, directed at himself as well as at those who antagonized him, was the most effective tool in confronting his particular social crisis. In his best-selling autobiography from 1964, *Nigger*, Gregory recalled an exchange in which he was taunted by a neighborhood friend about his father's perpetual absenteeism:

Hey, Gregory, where's your daddy these days?

Sure glad that motherfucker's out the house, got a little peace and quiet. Not like your house, York.

What you say?

Yeah, man, what a free show I had last night, better than the [movie theater], laying in bed with the window open, listening to your Daddy whop your Mommy. That was your Daddy, York, wasn't it?

When another friend intended to ridicule Gregory's cramped living space, he employed a less venomous but equally effective approach. To the potentially embarrassing question of just how many siblings he shared a bed with, Gregory replied: "Googobs of kids in my bed, man, when I get up to pee in the middle of the night gotta leave a bookmark so I don't lose my place."[1] For Gregory, the positive reactions by those around him proved that his mother had been right about there being "freedom in laughter."[2]

Young Bill Cosby, born and raised in Philadelphia, encountered similar taunting from peers. Reflecting on his school days in his 1991 book *Childhood*, Cosby recounted an incident in which a classmate and teacher initiated an embarrassing round of questioning after he wore a community league baseball uniform to school instead of traditional clothing. His odd choice of attire was very likely due to a lack of other clean clothing options, and the baseball uniform garnered twice the negative attention because of its extreme discoloration:

> "William," said my teacher, "does this look like Shibe Park to you?"
>
> "Oh no," I replied. "This is a school."
>
> "An excellent answer. So tell me: Why are you wearing a baseball uniform?"
>
> "Gee, I didn't know I had it on."
>
> "You mean you put it on by mistake?"
>
> "Yeah, that musta been it."
>
> And then she stared hard at me. "By the way, what *color* is that uniform?" To get the answer, I had to look down at myself, for my mother put something in her laundry that kept making the uniform a new color, or two or three; there were times I resembled the Hungarian flag.
>
> "What team you with?" said a boy named Calvin as we were walking out of the classroom. "The Boston *Pink* Sox?"

Based on these types of interactions, Cosby eventually learned the difference between people laughing *at* him versus *with* him. He worked to become a specialist at the latter. By the time he reached Mrs. McKinney's fifth-grade class, he knew how to maneuver himself into the role of entertainer rather than accept life as the butt of the joke. On the day Mrs. McKinney taught her class the art of storytelling and invited students to share personal stories that would entertain the entire group, Cosby immediately volunteered:

> "I got a story about sleepin' with my brother," [he] said.
>
> "You always sleep with your brother, William?"
>
> "Well, I get in bed with him, but there ain't much sleepin."
>
> "Fine, you come right up here and see if you can make a good story out of sleeping with your brother."

Instantly, young Cosby was at the front of the room using comedy to defuse the potentially embarrassing circumstance of sharing a bed with his younger brother:

> "I share a bed with my little brother, but he's not little enough. Y' see, he keeps touching me an' I don't like a bed that feels like a bus. An' sometimes, he does more than just *touch* me. He thinks the bed is a boxing ring, but he never goes to a neutral corner."

The laughter of his classmates pleased Cosby because it had not originated from someone else's attempt at ridicule. In fact, he credited the "sweet sound" his earliest storytelling induced as the "only vocational guidance I would ever need."[3]

Dick Gregory and Bill Cosby had remarkably similar experiences in their childhoods. With respect to race, class, gender, and even particular family dynamics, their lot was the same. Their urban environments, odd jobs, participation in organized sports, educational endeavors, and military experience bore striking parallels. As adolescents, they were separated by little more than geography and a small span of time.

Richard Claxton "Dick" Gregory was born October 12, 1932, in St. Louis, Missouri, to Presley and Lucille Gregory. The second of six children in a low-income, single-parent household, he experienced many of the hardships characteristic of urban families in the North. Food was scarce, beds and clothing were shared, and money was claimed by basic necessities.

On July 12, 1937, nearly five years after Gregory's birth, William Henry and Anna Pearl Cosby welcomed William Henry "Bill" Cosby Jr. to the world. Like the Gregorys, the Cosbys were familiar with economic hardship and developed a similar sustenance formula. Public assistance, informal systems of credit, benevolence from friends and neighbors, and income supplements provided by largely absentee fathers helped both households survive adverse circumstances. Both Gregory and Cosby grew up familiar with the difficulty and strain associated with life below the poverty line.

Gregory's St. Louis was a city that began the twentieth century with great promise. Its Civic League—a coalition of businessmen, politicians, and community leaders—initiated a "City Beautiful" program in the first decade of the twentieth century that soon provided parkways, public playgrounds and baths, a riverside drive, commercial development, and a new civic center. Initially, the improvement projects were inclusive enough to be enjoyed by all St. Louisans, including immigrants and African Americans. The city's mayor, Rolla Wells, was so proud of the widespread enjoyment that he credited the parks director with having "no caste prejudice," and he later wrote that the parks initiatives marked the first time the city's wealthy "mingled with" and showed "conscientious interest" in the poor and their recreational needs.[4] But widespread access to the city's public space accommodations did not translate into interracial harmony, as indicated by the savage race riot that occurred in East St. Louis on July 2, 1917, when white mobs burned, lynched, and shot African Americans in protest over the latter taking jobs vacated by white workers on strike. At least fifty people were killed in the affair known as the "Massacre at East St. Louis," and the total property damage was estimated at $1.4 million.[5]

At the time of Gregory's birth, residential segregation characterized the city. Although a federal judge had issued a permanent injunction in 1918 blocking a city-wide referendum that prevented any person of one race from moving to a block where 75 percent or more of the existing residents were of another race, de facto segregation continued throughout Gregory's childhood. This separation only intensified after World War I, as European immigration slowed and African Americans from the South migrated northward to answer the call of industries suffering labor shortages. The migrants sought escape from extreme racism and poverty. St. Louis railroad agents and city officials recruited African American laborers from the South with the promise of high wages and decent shelter, but they failed to deliver on both guarantees.[6] Nonetheless, the city's 1920 census reflected the rapid growth of its African American population.

From 43,960 in 1910 (6.4 percent of the total population), the number of African Americans in St. Louis rose to 69,854 (9 percent of the total population) by 1920.[7] When Gregory was born in 1932, the number of Black St. Louisans had reached 93,580 (11.4 percent of the total population).[8]

Like many African American women in the North, Lucille, Gregory's mother, earned a living as a domestic servant for a white family in a far more advantageous economic position. In his autobiography, Gregory recalled wondering just how she and the other African American women who left their neighborhoods at six o'clock each morning to iron, cook, and provide childcare for white people survived the physical and mental strain. He contemplated how his mother must have felt instructing white children to brush their teeth after meals and wash their hands after using the bathroom, while "she could never tell her own kids because there wasn't water or soap back home." Gregory knew that his mother was not alone in "wearing sacks over [her] shoes because it was so cold" while walking to and from a white family's home to help her own family survive.[9]

The Great Depression made life more difficult for nearly everyone, but St. Louis's African American population suffered a very severe economic setback. By the spring of 1933, the national unemployment rate was 24.9 percent; African American unemployment/underemployment in St. Louis was estimated at 80 percent (in comparison to roughly 30 percent among whites). Layoffs often concentrated on African American workers, increasing the number of jobs available for whites.[10] Coupled with the absence of any regular contributions to the household's bottom line by Gregory's father, Presley, the Gregory family suffered from poverty. Yet young Gregory's mother never allowed morale to sink. "We ain't poor, we just broke," Lucille Gregory taught. "Poor is a state of mind you never get out of, but being broke is just a temporary condition."[11]

Some of the material on Gregory's earliest comedy albums reconstructs the difficult circumstances of his childhood years created by the serious financial shortage in his home. When his mother would often refer to a biblical passage explaining that the meek will inherit the earth, young Gregory countered with the idea that the family should finally have a good meal before taking on a responsibility so large! In discussing the limited access to medical care for families such as his without the appropriate finances, Gregory further humored white audiences with a bit about falling ill as a child. Suffering from what he believed was double pneumonia, young Gregory asked his mother if she had called the doctor. When she explained that the goose grease she was applying to his chest would protect his health, young Gregory expressed doubt. If the ointment had any real value, he reasoned, then the goose it came from would not have died!

Because their family was so economically disadvantaged, the Gregory children often wore old and stained clothes. On one occasion, other parents in the neighborhood paid Gregory's mother a visit to inform her that Dick and his siblings were not acceptable playmates for their children. Embarrassed and disheartened, Gregory's mother demanded that her children stay home until she could afford to dress them in better clothes. Before leaving the house to work as a domestic in a white home, Mrs. Gregory also took the extreme measure of hiding all of her children's old clothes in an effort to keep them in the house. Unable to find their regular pants and shirts, young Gregory and his siblings dressed themselves in the only clothing items they could locate in the home—their mother's dresses, which had been given to her by "the rich white folks." Gregory recalled the experience in his 1964 autobiography: "The people laughed at us when we went outside in dresses, pointed and slapped their legs. We never played so good as we played that summer, with all those people watching us."[12]

Gregory demonstrated how life below the poverty line could be remembered with fondness. One of his favorite errands was going across the street for his mother to pick up grocery items from a store owned by "Mr. Ben," a white man generous enough to extend credit to Gregory's mother, albeit with exorbitant interest attached. Gregory discussed a particular visit to the store for a credit purchase of a loaf of bread:

> *Mr. Ben, mama want a loaf of bread—fresh bread.* And you know what kind he gonna give you, because the only kind of bread he buy from the bakery is that three-day old bread that he gets for nothing. At that time, bread was six cents a loaf. And you give him the [credit] book, and he opens it up, and he's fixing to [write] ninety-six cents, but he stops and he looks at you.
>
> He say: *Hey, lil Greg!* I say: *Yeah, Mr. Ben?*
>
> He say: *How you like school?* I say: *I like it.*
>
> *How you like math?* I say: *Oh, I love it!*

What's two and two? I say: *Four.*

Four and four? [I say:] *Eight.*

Fifty and fifty? [I say:] *A hundred.*

You're smart, huh?

So instead of [writing] ninety-six cents, he put forty-four cents down there. Now I'm mad, but it doesn't do me no good to get mad, because I know the minute I go home and say, *Mom, Mr. Ben charged us forty-four cents for a six-cents loaf of bread,* I know what she's gonna say. *Oh, he forgot to mark something down last week.*

But I didn't care about Mr. Ben putting forty-four cents down for a six-cents loaf of bread, because what he didn't realize is, when he went to get the loaf of bread, I wiped him out![13]

If taken literally, it is easy to identify a young, militant Gregory outsmarting a white merchant who profited at the expense of an economically disadvantaged African American community. However, given the tendency of humorists to exaggerate and fabricate stories for the sake of entertainment, such an analysis is risky. What can be determined quite clearly is the manner in which Gregory chose to look back on his childhood. He painted a picture of a crafty, rebellious adolescent aware of unfair treatment and motivated to strike back against that unfairness. This characterization of Gregory's childhood persona fits very well with the comedy act he had developed by 1962. It stands apart from Bill Cosby's more wholesome presentations of his childhood, even though little separates the comedians' actual backgrounds and experiences.

Bill Cosby was born in the Germantown residential district of Philadelphia, an area often referred to as "the Jungle" by its residents.[14] His family eventually settled into a first-floor apartment in the nearby Richard Allen Homes, a residential development designed to upgrade the older, substandard living spaces of many African Americans in Philadelphia. Named in recognition of Bishop Richard Allen, the clergyman who founded the African Methodist Episcopal Church, the Richard Allen Homes were among a handful of essentially segregated housing projects supported through New Deal funding initiatives between 1936 and 1940. Yet the two new communities within that handful that targeted the residential needs of African Americans—the Richard Allen and James Weldon Johnson Homes—were not nearly enough to meet demand.

The financial gift of Benjamin and Pearl Mason, an African American couple who lived on relief before winning $150,000 in the Grand National Steeplechase Sweepstakes in 1940, demonstrates the state of housing for African Americans in Philadelphia during Cosby's toddler years. Rather than enjoy the full amount of their winnings, the Masons invested $80,000 in building the Frances Plaza Apartments for fellow African Americans in desperate need of decent housing. Mrs. Mason delivered a particularly telling set of instructions on behalf of future residents at Frances Plaza to Raymond Pace Alexander, a well-known African American attorney with whom she entrusted her and her husband's funds:

> They got to get theyselves homes where the roof don't leak . . . God has given me a concern for my people. Now you take the sweepstakes money and build some homes. The rain water been pouring through the roof all my life. I never had a inside toilet. My kids have to play in the alley and get theyselves cool in summer under a fireplug. I want green grass and flowers, too. I never did have no flowers. They's got to be a fountain where the kids can fuss around and play and not be getting hit by no automobiles.[15]

While Mrs. Mason's design requests resulted in nearly 40 percent of the land acquired for the construction of Frances Plaza being left open for recreation, the architects of the Richard Allen Homes made no such accommodations. Cosby made light of the limited public space available to children who grew up in his neighborhood in a 1966 bit called "The Playground":

> I have definite proof that the grownups were trying to get rid of us. For what reason, I'm not sure. It might have been the fact that they had no babysitters. It's very expensive to watch us. I'll proceed to prove my point.
>
> First of all, we had a perfectly good playground. It was a field leveled off. They tore down some houses. We called it our

playground. There was broken glass and rocks and bricks and everything on it. We never lost one kid. Not one kid died. Not one broken arm, broken leg, broken anything. Maybe a little gash here and there, but that's alright. And then the grownups started in. They moved in the monkey bars. The monkey bars came in, [and] we lost 124 kids in one day.

Hey, look at me. I'm on top of the—[imaginary scream of a child falling]. Kids were falling off the monkey bars like snowflakes, breaking arms, legs, losing everything, hanging upside down. I never played on them myself because I saw the kids falling off of them. And I tried to warn them.

Please, don't play on the mon—[imaginary scream of a child falling]. There goes another one. And I made it my philosophy after that never to play on nothin' I saw no grownups playing on!

Cosby offered an additional tale that suggests that neighborhood streets were common locations for play in his childhood experience:

We played street football, right there on the street, and this is where we had the greatest quarterback in the world. Our quarterback, he had to control twenty-three men on the side, and he was really great at it. You women don't know anything about it. You played with dolls and stuff like that, but here's a guy with an ingenious mind. He'd call a football play like this. He'd always get down on one knee and draw up things. He'd take a coke bottle top:

Now, Shorty, this is you. This is the coke bottle.

[Shorty:] I don't wanna be the coke bottle today.

OK, what do you wanna be?

[Shorty:] *I wanna be the piece of glass.*

OK. Now listen to this. Barney, go down ten steps and cut left behind the black Chevy. Philbert, you run down to my house, and wait in the living room. Cosby, you go down to Third Street, catch the J bus, have [the driver] open the doors at Nineteenth Street, [and] I'll fake it to ya.

There was always that one fat kid they'd never throw it to who says, "What about me?"

[Quarterback:] *You go long.*

We had a lot of good plays going like that. *I'll throw it over the water tower. You'll catch it as it bounces off.*[16]

Cosby's presentation of his childhood gives a clear indication of his familiarity with poverty in the urban north, but it stands apart from Gregory's. It masks their similar backgrounds because the style and content of his stage material is less biting than Gregory's. Cosby's childhood remembrances are void of the bitterness and victimization by class and race often explored by Gregory. As a result, their adult personas and experiences as youth appear in far greater contrast than actually was the case.

Cosby and his younger brother, Russell, often referred to their father, William Cosby Sr., as "the Giant." By the time the Giant left his family for good, he had left permanent reminders of his failures as a husband and father. Having turned to drinking and gambling in response to the pressures of work and family, he sometimes responded violently when Anna Cosby refused to drop her requests for money to help with rent, food, and household supplies. Young Cosby and his siblings were tortured by the "sudden sound of sickening violence, followed by the softer sound of sobbing" on the nights when the Giant had heard enough from his wife. Cosby carried the emotional trauma into adulthood, as he once explained that he and his brothers equated the word "father" with "disappointment."[17]

Gregory's father, Presley "Big Prez" Gregory, was also a man prone to violence, and his victims also included women. On a Christmas Eve during Gregory's youth, Big Prez strode into the home after a long absence. He had no gifts. He had spent the previous hours drinking at a local tavern, and it was not long before a familiar scene erupted:

He beat her all through the house, every room, swinging his belt and whopping her with his hand and cussing her and kicking her and knocking her down and telling her all about his women.

"Think you're so goddamn good, bitch," said my Daddy, cracking my Momma across her back with his belt. She whimpered and fell against a little table, knocking over a lamp from the white folks. She bent over to pick up the lamp and Big Prez kicked her in the backside and she fell forward on the linoleum floor. She lay there, her face pressed against the linoleum, sobbing.

He grabbed her hair and pulled her up to her knees. Momma looked up at him, tears running down her cheeks. Slap. Right across her face. "I got bitches, women like you never seen, proud to walk down the street with Big Prez." Slap. Momma fell down on her face again.[18]

The manner in which Gregory and Cosby shared the domestic violence they witnessed as youths is further evidence of the differing presentations of their pasts. While Gregory proved comfortable revealing sensitive and graphic details, Cosby took a more reserved approach. After Cosby became a major celebrity and was asked if his childhood was a happy one, he responded, "It will be, onstage."[19] Unlike Gregory's uncensored presentation of life below the poverty line and dysfunctional family situations, Cosby carefully constructed his image of his past, intending to soften the harsh realities of his earlier experiences.

Cosby's mother, Anna, who considered him a "good boy," worked as a domestic servant in Philadelphia throughout his adolescent years.[20] Like many thousands of African Americans in Philadelphia, she did not earn an income that could provide adequately for her children. From 1910 to 1930, a period highlighted by World War I and the migration of millions of African Americans from the South to the North, Philadelphia's African American population grew from 84,450 (5.5 percent) to 219,599 (11.3 percent).[21] Lured by the promise of better social opportunities and higher wages, most of these newer Philadelphians, if employed at all, served alongside older African American residents in unskilled labor positions throughout the Depression era.[22] Employment opportunities did not improve significantly for African Americans until the World War II period. Anna Cosby, however, found no upgrade from her role as a domestic servant in the late 1940s, and her family depended on government relief.

"The only thing I had to give him . . . was plenty of love," Cosby's mother said. One of the more influential practices that Anna conducted in her home was reading stories to her children. Cosby remembered being "scared to death" while listening to his mother read the adventures of Mark Twain's characters, and credited those tales with serving as one of his major comic influences.[23] Cosby tested out his skill at replicating the style of comedy heard in his home so much that Charles Moritz speculated that "even as a child, [he] was a comedian."[24] A sixth-grade report card from Mary Channing Wister Elementary School in Philadelphia indicated that Cosby "feels it is his mission to amuse his classmates in and out of school." Similar to Gregory's use of humor to gain and defend his social standing among peers, Cosby explored the comedic talent unknowingly nurtured by his mother in order to fit in with those around him. "I got to feeling that as long as people were laughing, they were my friends," he remembered. "So to get myself across and to be an important person, I made them laugh. Through humor, I gained acceptance."[25]

Well before stand-up comedy, the first job Gregory and Cosby had in common was shining shoes. Although Cosby received more formalized training as an apprentice in a Philadelphia shoe shop, his experience earning nickels and dimes from customers was similar to Gregory's. In his autobiography, Gregory described a violent incident that erupted in a St. Louis tavern while shining the shoes of a white female customer. Perhaps intoxicated, the woman used young Gregory to deride the sexual capability of her white male companion based on the size of his genitalia: "Heard these little coons are hung like horses, I'm getting tired of you worms." After overhearing the woman's continued banter, another white male patron hopped off of a nearby barstool and kicked Gregory in the face for his role in having prompted a white woman to make such statements. "For Christ's sake, he's just a little kid," an uninvolved white male said. Gregory was asked not to return to shine shoes at the tavern. While the extent to which the incident is truthful cannot be known, it is no accident that Cosby's stage material and writings are absent such chilling encounters, particularly those involving race. His interest in presenting a wholesome adolescent experience that resonated with mainstream audiences prevented him from sharing any dramatic, cruel episodes with whites whose shoes he shined.

Both Gregory and Cosby displayed above-average athletic talent. The sport in which they commonly excelled was track and field. Gregory's initial motivation for running was quite unique—he set out to join the track team because it presented the opportunity to shower every evening after school. At Sumner High School in St. Louis, he quickly rose from a kid with no locker or uniform to one of the strongest, fastest distance runners in the state. Helping his mother financially nearly derailed his track career. When the Korean War opened up employment opportunities in defense industries, seventeen-year-old Gregory claimed to be twenty-one to qualify for a job at an ammunition plant. He soon earned as much as $200 per week, a salary that helped transform his family's lifestyle:

> I could walk home at the end of the week and put money in Momma's hand. We could go shopping with cash instead of the green tablet; we could walk into a supermarket instead of Mister Ben's. I could stand at the check-out counter and listen to the cash register and my heart didn't jump with every ring. Momma could pay back some bills and buy some new second-hand furniture and some clothes, and not have to go to the white folks' every day.

When Gregory began to recognize that his second- and third-place finishes might result in more first-place finishes had he not been so tired from working, and that he could very well become the "great runner" his coach saw in him if he spent more time training, he told his mother he wanted to quit his job. Lucille Gregory probably dreaded the loss of her son's income. Nonetheless, she gave her blessing to his desire to forego the role of breadwinner and return to being a teenager.

Running allowed Gregory to concentrate on his personal thoughts. He enjoyed running for miles each day until the pain in his legs alerted him to stop. The regimen proved successful. In the spring of 1951, during his junior year of high school, Gregory placed first in the one-mile race at the Missouri state meet for African American runners. When the state's annual track and field book was published later that fall, Gregory was upset that his name and time in the one-mile event—one of the fastest in the state among high school runners of all races—was not included. *The St. Louis Argus*, a weekly African American newspaper, was the only publication that recorded Gregory's accomplishment.[26]

On September 29, 1951, members of the Parents-Teachers Association (PTA) at Sumner High School participated in a march protesting overcrowded African American schools in St. Louis. Gregory attended the event with an admittedly selfish motive—he was just as determined to draw attention to his omission from the annual track and field book as he was to complain about overcrowded classrooms. The press covering the march listened to the frustration of Harry L. Brown, president of Sumner's PTA, who demanded that white schools be converted to African American use to help alleviate congestion.[27] They also heard Gregory's complaint about having his impressive finish in the one-mile race overlooked. "That year I became an activist for change," he recalled.[28]

Gregory performed well when Sumner High began participating in integrated track and field and cross-country meets during his senior year. Decades of segregation had led to faulty assumptions from runners on both sides of the racial divide. Gregory and his teammates believed their white counterparts received "special conditioning and food" that placed them at an advantage for distance running. A rumor among their white competitors was that African American teams required only three members to amass enough points to finish first at meets: "one would win the 100 and the 220; the second would win both hurdles, and the third would win both the half and the mile. Then the three regulars would borrow a Negro water boy and win the relays." Gregory upheld suspicions of his athletic prowess by winning the first integrated cross-country meet, which he ran on a trail in Wood River, Missouri. He gloated upon seeing his name in all the white newspapers the next day and followed up with more brilliant performances. He became a state champion after finishing first at an integrated cross-country meet held at Forest Park in St. Louis and won second place in a fifteen-mile race as the only high school runner in a field of college boys. Gregory soon abused his increased popularity by skipping team practices, staying out late, and drinking beer. In the final meet of his senior season, he placed a disappointing seventeenth. "The coach was mad and the press was disgusted and I was ashamed," he remembered.[29] Nevertheless, he had carved out an impressive high school career as a distance runner.

With the assistance of his coach, an alumnus of Southern Illinois University (SIU) in Carbondale, Gregory enrolled at the institution in the fall of 1952 and resumed his excellent running. He became captain of the track team, broke a state record by running the half-mile race in one minute and fifty-four seconds, and won the university's Outstanding Athlete award as a sophomore in 1953. Gregory remembered that the only perks his minor celebrity status in the town did not provide were eating out with white teammates and sitting in the orchestra section of the movie theater. The latter proved surprising because of his background in

St. Louis: "I lived in a Negro neighborhood, went to a Negro school, and the only white people I knew were those makin' money on the Negro," he recalled, "and *they* loved us."[30] Gregory had grown up watching films in his segregated neighborhood where he and other youth sat in the balcony by choice. He perhaps should have reasoned that the Varsity movie theater would be spatially segregated, but he did not. When he and a female companion sat in the orchestra section near Gregory's white teammates one evening, a "racial baptism" ensued.[31]

First, several whites stared and pointed, although Gregory assumed it was because they recognized him as a track star. Next, a white usher who was a fellow student at SIU offered a stern suggestion that Gregory reseat himself and his date in the balcony. "That's okay, baby, I'll sit here tonight," he said. Finally, after the manager called the police, Gregory left the theater with his crying date, who had known better than to challenge Jim Crow. "Be sure and get your money back," the manager said. "Keep it. I'll be back," Gregory responded. When he went back alone the next evening, the theater allowed him to sit at orchestra level. On subsequent nights when he showed up with other African American students from SIU, the theater again allowed them to sit at orchestra level. The manager soon pulled Gregory into his office for a candid discussion. He explained that he had paid dearly for a Hollywood film about Jesus called *The Robe* and that the loss of white customers would force him into bankruptcy. If Gregory would refrain from sitting in the orchestra section while *The Robe* played at the theater, then African American moviegoers would be allowed to sit anywhere they desired immediately afterward. Gregory agreed.[32]

The role Gregory played in ending segregated seating at the Varsity theater in Carbondale is intriguing. Were his actions part of a broader movement, or did he single-handedly organize one of the earliest successful sit-ins of the civil rights era? If the latter is true, then what was the source of his activism? Years of playing "the dozens" certainly prepared him to respond to antagonism rather than retreat from it. But many other African American children, including Bill Cosby, endured similar confrontations that did not result in the same initiative. Gregory's participation in a 1951 march protesting separate and unequal schools appears to be the most likely catalyst for his decision to recruit other African American students to challenge Jim Crow at the Varsity theater. Finally, to what extent should Gregory be trusted as a source? He publicized details of events fewer than ten years after they occurred—a reasonable period for a young man's memory to remain intact. Yet Gregory was an established celebrity comedian by 1964 whose shtick was confronting racism with intelligent humor. There was professional incentive to aggrandize his role in integrating the Varsity theater. In either case, there is no similar experience or idea posited by Cosby in the arena of civil rights activism as a high school or college student.

The involvement of the United States in Cold War politics interrupted Gregory's collegiate experience. After being drafted into the Army and serving stateside from 1954 to 1956, he returned to SIU with reduced motivation to compete as a runner. He had participated in competitive track in the Army but could no longer figure out "what [he] was running for" by the time he returned to Carbondale.[33] Although Gregory held strong social connections at SIU as a member of the band and Alpha Phi Alpha fraternity, he left the university without a degree less than a year following his military experience, telling friends and campus administrators the "premature truth" that he was headed for stardom after accepting a $25,000 job offer from the mayor of Baltimore.[34] Gregory had met the son of Baltimore Mayor Frank D'Alesandro while in the Army, but the report of a job offer was a complete fabrication. It was easier than explaining that he was dropping out of college with no solid plan. He chose Chicago as his destination in the fall of 1956 because his older brother lived in the city. Gregory spent several months working at the U.S. Post Office and Ford Aircraft before dedicating himself to comedy in 1958.

Cosby's young adult experiences are very similar to Gregory's, although notable differences exist. Cosby did not enjoy the popularity of being a star athlete while at Central High School in Philadelphia. He scored high enough on an IQ exam to gain admission to the all-male college preparatory school, which had only a 7 percent African American student population, but soon transferred to Germantown High School, where the racial divide was about equal. "Germantown High had some girls at least!" he quipped.[35] The change proved ineffective. Cosby dropped out of Germantown after being held back in the tenth grade. Education for African American students in Philadelphia was in a crisis at the time of his withdrawal. Fifty-two percent of all African American boys who began public school in Philadelphia in 1949 failed to eventually graduate, and vocational education became the solution to "enable children who did not thrive in academic courses to remain in school and receive a diploma" while improving their employment prospects. By 1963, seven years after Cosby's withdrawal, 76 percent of African American students in Philadelphia's public school system pursued "the nonacademic curricula, mainly the trade and commercial tracks." The small population of African American students at Central may have factored into Cosby's decision to quit school even after transferring. One study suggested that African American boys' underrepresentation at campuses such as Central in the 1950s contributed to "their greater likelihood of getting jobs before they finished high school." Other factors linked to Philadelphia's alarming dropout rate for African American students included inadequate funding, overcrowding, poor quality of instruction, and difficult home environments.[36]

As a nineteen-year-old dropout, Cosby first shined shoes and then took a job fixing auto mufflers to earn money. He found the long-term prospects of both as unappealing as the low-skilled jobs and criminal activities taken up by many of the young men around him. Cosby's alternative plan was enlisting in the Navy. In 1956, the year Gregory ended his two-year draft enlistment with the Army, Cosby began training as a Navy hospital corpsman.[37] "I entered the service after I graduated high school because the dropouts already had the jobs," he told an all-white audience in 1965.[38] The intentionally misleading joke elicited a huge round of laughter and went a step beyond Lawrence Mintz's assertion that "the comedian must establish *for the audience* that the group is homogenous, a community, if the laughter is to come easily."[39] Cosby's presentation of himself as a high school graduate signified the importance of *his* inclusion in the homogenization process. He masked the sobering realism of entering the Navy as a high school dropout to lessen the difference already present in his racial "otherness."

Both Gregory and Cosby struggled with the individual discipline required of Army and Navy men, respectively. "I overslept almost every day," Gregory remembered.[40] Cosby recalled similar difficulty meeting his required wake-up time and other expectations. After being told that he needed to report for breakfast at "zero four thirty," he purportedly replied, "*In the morning?*" Cosby further detailed his trouble with waking up so early:

> The man woke us up [at] zero four thirty. You can't see outside. So you go in, you clean up, fall out. It's pitch black except for one light to the mess hall. I said to the man, "Listen, I can save the taxpayers money. *Don't wake me up.*"[41]

Cosby spent the majority of his Navy tour working with servicemen injured in the Korean War. He was stationed at Quantico, Virginia, followed by an assignment to the Bethesda Naval Hospital in Maryland. He made a brief sail from Newfoundland to Guantanamo Bay in Cuba before finally being assigned to the Philadelphia Naval Hospital.[42] Cosby credited his observations of Navy men working hard to better themselves as the source of his newfound maturity and desire for self-improvement. Many of them struggled through coursework that came easily to him; he realized that he had been cheating himself. "I thought about how these guys were suffering to learn and how much of a sin it was for me, who had a better intelligence, to be doing nothing," he recalled.[43] He earned his high school diploma after participating in a special program for servicemen.

Like Gregory, Cosby excelled in competitive track and field. He posted a time of 10.2 seconds in the hundred-yard dash and finished seventeenth in the nation in the high jump event at a competition sponsored by the Amateur Athletic Union (AAU).[44] Cosby got along well with his white teammates. However, when they traveled south for track competitions in the late 1950s and early 1960s, they were reminded of America's hard racial divide. Cosby suffered the indignity of entering restaurants through back doors and dining in kitchen areas with African American workers rather than his white teammates at southern diners.[45] It was a "racial baptism" that he made light of in later interviews. The "well-stocked refrigerator" was at his full disposal when he sat in the kitchen, and he enjoyed his "place of honor crowned with a royal feast of cold cuts all piled high in a giant hero sandwich." Some of Cosby's white teammates made light of the situation as well. They joked about his "special treatment" when he returned to the bus with the tail end of a giant sandwich and asked for future invitations to the kitchen area where the seemingly unlimited supply of food was located.[46]

Cosby's athletic ability translated into success in other sports. He played football and basketball during his enlistment. His physical gifts and promise as a twenty-two-year-old Navy veteran earned him a scholarship to Temple University in 1961. He chose physical education as his major because he envisioned a future as a gym coach: "I wanted to save seventh- and eighth-grade boys from what happened to me."[47] Cosby's determination fueled his progress in the classrooms and sports arenas at Temple. He lettered in track and earned the nickname "Riggie" because of the onset of rigor mortis he often complained to his coach about due to his workload anchoring the relay squad, high-jumping, shot-putting, and discus throwing—all of which were in addition to his membership on the football and basketball teams.[48] Cosby won the Middle Atlantic Coast championship in the high jump event as a twenty-three-year-old freshman and continued to perform well into his junior year. But financial strain tugged at Cosby throughout his time at Temple. His scholarship did not cover room and board, so he found work as a bartender to earn money. The thrill of entertaining customers while serving drinks opened Cosby's mind to the possibility of life as a full-time comedian. Like Gregory, he decided to leave college before graduation and try his luck at making it in the real world.

In the early 1960s, white America would be formally introduced to Gregory and Cosby, African American stand-up comedians with remarkably similar backgrounds yet dramatically different acts. Both young men successfully transitioned from poor college dropouts to American cultural icons, although many who enjoyed their performances may not have imagined that their prior experiences were strikingly similar. As the nation experienced landmark political and social changes in the 1960s, Gregory and Cosby spearheaded a paradigm shift in the arena of comedy. Their respective rises to stardom in mainstream America included challenges, triumphs, and controversies shaped by the Civil Rights Movement. These two young men, each in his own way, treated it as a laughing matter.

Chapter 2

Coming to the Stage

Dick Gregory's debut comedy album, *In Living Black & White*, was marketed to American consumers in 1961 by Colpix Records. Company executives took notice of "the first Negro comedian to make his way into the nightclub scene big-time" after his appearance on the *Jack Paar Show* and feature in *Time Magazine*.[1] They delivered Gregory a $25,000 advance for two albums. Alex Dreier, a Chicago-based news reporter, narrated and wrote the liner notes for the first album. His remarks were clearly intended to introduce the African American comedian to a white mainstream: "Dick Gregory is neither Ralph Bunche, nor Amos and Andy. He is not Uncle Tom, come to amuse the 'white folks' with his native negro humor, nor is he a brassy intruder, stamping his foot for your attention and denouncing you bitterly if he does not get it."[2] Dreier's summary helped prepare white consumers for the subtle yet calculated attacks against white supremacy delivered within the album's first few minutes:

> A lot of people don't understand how we can own so many Cadillacs with them inferior jobs. Well, racial segregation buys us Cadillacs. You have a country club you can join, but I can't, so I save $500 a year. You know damn well I'm not taking my family to Florida this winter; that's another $1500 I save. Walk out of here tonight and get hit by a bus, I'm not going to the best hospital where they gonna charge me $2500, so I go to city hospital for *free*. Figure it up: I save $2500 plus [$2000]. General Motors will sell me anything I want![3]

A review of Gregory's first album in the *New York Times* concluded, "he is all they say he is." The article distinguished Gregory from earlier African American comedic entertainers, suggesting that he possessed an "acid of resentment" that could pop up at any time from any angle to keep his audience "alert and 'honest.'"[4] It was an accurate assessment. Gregory peppered his act with racial material that highlighted the injustices of segregation and Jim Crow. He gained respect for his professionalism, intelligence, and audacity as he became the Jackie Robinson of stand-up comedy.

Cosby's introduction to mainstream America in 1963 required less buffering. His debut comedy album, *Bill Cosby Is a Very Funny Fellow, Right!*, included no mention of race, segregation, or inequality. The approximately thirty-minute recording of Cosby's live performance at the Bitter End nightclub in New York City's Greenwich Village simply highlighted his masterful timing, storytelling, and audience command. This classic presentation of his comedic talent received a nomination for a Grammy Award in 1964.[5] Allan Sherman, a fellow entertainer widely known for his hit single, "Hello Muddah, Hello Fadduh," wrote the liner notes. He communicated to buyers that Cosby "would be funny if he were green or purple or chartreuse." Sherman further explained that Cosby "is so good that what he has is more than talent; he has the gift of comedy. He has something that makes you feel delight when you're with him . . . in an office, in a nightclub, or standing on a street corner. He has joy in being alive, and he communicates it to you, so that when you're with him, you too are glad you're alive."[6] Listeners were rewarded with Cosby's charm and charisma as he discussed topics ranging from the peculiarities of superheroes to the differences between men and women.

The universal themes in Cosby's humor widened his appeal beyond the boundaries of race, class, gender, geography, and age. His material was as suitable for a family at home after dinner as it was for a couple out for a night on the town. Cosby's act also met the approval of Lyndon B. Johnson. In May of 1964, he was booked for two political fundraisers billed as a salute to the president. Mahalia Jackson, Joan Baez, and Woody Allen were among several other scheduled entertainers. Richard Adler, show producer for both events, recalled reviewing the entertainment lineup with President Johnson. "I spoke with him to make sure there was nobody he didn't like," Adler said.[7] Following a trail blazed by Gregory, Cosby had arrived.

Most white Americans who saw Gregory's and Cosby's earliest live performances and listened to their first comedy records viewed the professional stand-up comedians as instant celebrities. Yet few outside Chicago were aware of Gregory's years of experience as a stand-up comedian prior to his groundbreaking crossover performances in the early 1960s. His astounding success in all-white venues paved the way for Cosby's rapid advance from a local star in Philadelphia to a widely known celebrity. Other African American comedians who began their careers in the 1960s also benefited from Gregory's unprecedented dialogue with white America. "Dick Gregory was the greatest, and he was the first," Richard Pryor remembered. "Somebody had to break down that door."[8]

Gregory began crafting his skills in stand-up comedy by entering amateur shows at SIU and Army bases.[9] His troublesome behavior as an enlisted man served as an unlikely catalyst for one of his first high-stakes appearances onstage. While serving on "Kitchen Patrol," Gregory once stepped into a huge serving pot and took a nap. A colonel became aware of Gregory's antics and ordered him to make good on his propensity for foolishness. "You are either a great comedian or a goddamned malingerer," the colonel determined. "There is an open talent show at the service club tonight. You will go down there, and you will win it." Gregory had finally received an order that he was eager to obey. He won the talent show by telling one-liners about the military experience: "I told them how the Army charged me eighty-five dollars when I lost my rifle. That's why in the Navy the captain always goes down with his ship."[10]

Gregory was soon added to the Army's Special Services tour as an entertainer. After delivering variety performances that included "clowning around and playing the bongos and singing a few calypso songs," he developed longer stand-up routines. He recalled branching off and performing at an African American nightclub in Virginia. "I never really prepared for those shows," Gregory said. In 1955, he competed at an all-Army show for a chance to perform on *The Ed Sullivan Show*. He did not win, but he viewed his lack of success in that instance as a blessing in disguise: "I would have had the wrong attitude. I probably would have never worked as hard as I did later."[11]

Gregory entered the professional entertainment arena in January 1958 more than a year after dropping out of SIU. He began his career in comedy after attending a nightclub show in Chicago and paying the emcee five dollars for stage time. Modest success encouraged Gregory to pay for stage time the following week at another nightclub, the Esquire Show Lounge. His performance there drew such a favorable response that the owner offered Gregory a salary of ten dollars a night to serve as the weekend emcee. "It's one thing to be funny when you're a guest on another man's stage, something else again when it's your stage and you have to be funny night after night," Gregory remembered. Initially he "wasn't funny at all," but his preparation for stardom had begun.[12]

Training for success was a serious endeavor that distinguished Gregory throughout his career. He spent the majority of each week preparing material for his weekend shows. Comedy records, books, magazines, TV shows, and banter among friends became sources for professional development. The couple from whom he rented a room often listened to his routines and provided feedback.[13] Gregory's work ethic provided him with a considerable following just months after he began. A pre–Fourth-of-July ball at the nightclub was advertised as "Starring the Hilarious Dick Gregory and His All-Review."[14] Gregory's success inclined him to seek a raise later in the year from ten dollars to twelve dollars a night. "I told them if they didn't give me a two dollar raise I'd quit on them," he remembered. "They didn't give me a raise."[15]

Out of work, Gregory experienced feelings similar to those he had after dropping out of SIU. An uncertain path lay before him. Gregory's hunger for the challenge of infusing an audience with humor must have increased, but every day out of the spotlight placed more distance between him and that feeling of gratification that comes after a good set. Absent this thrill that so many comedians chase and continually seek to top, Gregory likely experienced depression. "Toward Christmas," he recalled, "I played a couple of benefits, just to make me feel I was still an entertainer."[16] He served as emcee for a "Turkey Party" hosted by the C and C Lounge in Chicago. The four-day affair featured a variety of acts, including Chicagoan Norman Simmons and his band.[17] Gregory also joined the Gala Holiday Ball lineup at a new entertainment venue, Club Evergreen.[18] It was during one of these benefit shows that Gregory learned of a vacant former nightclub fifteen miles south of Chicago. After locating the elderly owner of the building and negotiating lease arrangements, he became a manager as well as a comedian.

The Apex Club in Robbins, Illinois, experienced a brief renaissance under Gregory's direction. In January 1959, the *Chicago Defender* reported it as being "back on the scene" and "very popular with Chicagoans who like driving into the far southside of Chicago district for nightly entertainment, drinks and meals."[19] Praise for Gregory and his new venture continued into the early spring. "In Dick Gregory the Apex boasts one of the best young comics of the season. His antics are of the side cracking variety and always fresh material," the *Defender* noted in March.[20] By June, the success of the nightclub appeared certain. It was billed as "one of the most popular summer spots in middlewest."[21] It seemed that Gregory's decision to leave the Esquire Show Club after management failed to grant his request for a two-dollar raise was a brilliant move. However, the Apex was not as successful as it appeared.

"It's impossible to be in the night-club business for six months and never make a penny. Absolutely impossible," Gregory vented. "I'll never believe it happened to me." His fresh comic material had been appropriately recognized. The topical humor he brought to the stage after scanning newspapers and magazines proved effective. But Gregory's diligence and resourcefulness were not enough to turn a profit after paying for advertising, utilities, liquor, and salaries for performers and club staff. Gregory's retelling of a robbery attempt conveys the Apex Club's dire financial circumstances:

> The second week in May, a man walked into the Apex Club with a gun. There were six customers in the club that night, and they jumped up and ran out. The waitresses and the bandsmen acts flattened out against the walls and froze when he walked around the tables, kicking chairs out of his way and waving the gun at the girl behind the money drawer. I came down off the stage and walked right up to him and looked him right in the eyes.
> "Look, mister, you don't know what I've been through, or you wouldn't come in here with that gun, you'd come with money."[22]

Gregory later claimed to say to the would-be robber that "you need to pull a gun and shoot me to run me out of here," which makes it questionable whether there was a gun or even a robbery attempt.[23] Nevertheless, the club had unsustainable costs. Gregory lost the Apex in July. The elderly woman from whom he leased the building decided to resume ownership and capitalize on its rebirth once he fell too far behind in rent payments. Entertainment shows may not have been a part of the venue after July. The last mention of the Apex in the press came in September 1959. It was listed among several other Chicago establishments as a place where African Americans could find "food of the home cooking variety."[24]

Gregory returned to his former position as emcee at the Esquire Show Lounge for the same ten-dollar salary. But he again walked away from the lounge after being offered an emcee position at a nightclub owned by Herman Roberts, the African American "cafe baron" whose self-named nightclub was the largest, most successful venue in Chicago featuring African American entertainers.[25] Gregory's fortunes tumbled when he learned that the Roberts Show Club changed emcees every four weeks. The $125 salary he had asked for and received was only temporary. With his new wife, Lillian, who had depleted her finances supporting the Apex Club, and infant daughter, Michele, Gregory zipped around Chicago looking for a place to resume his career. He took odd jobs along the way to supplement Lillian's income as a secretary at the University of Chicago. He performed at the Monday night auditions hosted by the American Guild of Variety Artists (AGVA). The white nightclub owners and agents repeatedly asked Gregory if he could sing or dance while evaluating his appropriateness for their white patrons. He consistently replied, "I'm a comedian, sir."[26]

Gregory's response marks an important moment in the African American comic tradition. African American humor had first been presented to the American mainstream in the form of minstrelsy—an entertainment style that "transformed and parodied" African American humor for the amusement of whites—in the mid-1800s.[27] It featured white entertainers in blackface (black facial makeup) who ridiculed the language, appearance, mannerisms, and intelligence of African Americans to make the race appear ignorant and foolish. It lasted for more than fifty years. African American entertainers who worked in the early 1900s often adopted the minstrel style, including the blackface appearance, to appease white promoters and audiences. Their acts continued the presentation of African American buffoonery across a wide network of entertainment venues known as the vaudeville circuit. Will Rogers, a legendary white comedian, helped advance stand-up comedy during the vaudeville era by offering "astute and political commentary." Other white comics, such as Bob Hope, George Burns, and Gracie Allen, joined the evolution from variety performers into professional comedians.[28] African Americans, however, were granted no such license to drop the "depravity, venality, and ignorance that characterized minstrel humor" while entertaining white audiences.[29] Following the decline of vaudeville in the 1930s, they instead evolved into professional stand-up comedians in the 1940s and 1950s while entertaining African American audiences in small theaters and rooms across the nation.

White owners and agents had asked Gregory if he could perform vaudeville-type song and dance routines in addition to comedy bits because they helped reinforce America's social order of "white over black." They comforted whites by providing familiar sounds and movements—commonly referred to as "shuckin' and jivin' "—between their lighthearted jokes. Gregory's insistence on employment as a professional stand-up comedian, one hired for the sole purpose of entertaining predominantly white audiences with topical material from his own point of view, was ahead of its time. Club owners and agents feared his act may have provided too much of a shock to white patrons based on his divergence in style from other African American solo acts.

Timmie Rogers, Slappy White, and Nipsey Russell had humored white audiences with comedy bits in the 1950s, but their popularity was based on the variety feature of their acts, not their stage material. Rogers was nearly fired once after showing up to work a two-week gig in a dinner jacket rather than a colorful zoot suit costume. A club owner had previously booked Rogers upon observing him in a two-man act, and he assumed the green and red zoot suit worn by Rogers was part of his shtick. "Where's that suit?" the owner asked. "Gone down the drain," Rogers answered. "You put that suit back on," he was told, "or you haven't got a job."[30] Although Rogers was permitted to work (he was fired after one week), he experienced a familiar reminder of the Sambo-like presentation many white club owners expected of African American comedic performers. Gregory's demand for pay based on his brand of intelligent humor was a rejection of this norm. He was a pioneer for a new generation of African American stand-up comedians who offered neither "a passively slumped shoulder while delivering a punchline, an overly exaggerated widening of the eyes, [nor] an apprehensive glance in search of approval from non-black crowds."[31]

White stand-up comedy experienced another revolution in the 1950s. Comedians of this era introduced material that was "more personal, observational, and point-of-view driven" than those who came before them. White comedians of the prior era, such as Jack Benny, Milton Berle, and Bob Hope, focused more on style rather than content, and they tended to "plow through established and generic themes (for instance, mother-in-law jokes or ethnic jokes)."[32] Mort Sahl was the first to represent the new breed of white comedian in the 1950s. Gerald Nachman wrote that Sahl was "a whirlwind whose ideas defined him; behind each joke lurked a sharply etched, cynical worldview."[33] Sahl made his stand-up comedy debut at the "hungry i" nightclub in San Francisco in 1955. It took him only three weeks to find his groove as a socially conscious, "aggressively virile" comedian who walked onstage carrying a folded newspaper.[34] He blazed the trail for white satirists, such as Lenny Bruce, and helped condition mainstream America to accept intelligent and sharp social criticism from stand-up comedians. Gregory often fielded questions about being compared to Mort Sahl. Instead of reporters referring to him as an "African American Mort Sahl," Gregory reasoned, perhaps they should have referred to Sahl as a "white Dick Gregory."[35]

Gregory's career sputtered for more than a year following his declaration to the AGVA that he was not a variety performer. He was in and out of Roberts Show Club as a guest emcee, and he once sat among the club's predominantly white audience who turned out to see Nipsey Russell open for Sammy Davis Jr. The experience, among others, led Gregory to ponder his response to a white audience member heckling him with the word "nigger." It happened during one of his irregular gigs in 1960 at a white, working-class club on the outskirts of Chicago. Gregory recalled: "The audience froze, and I wheeled around without batting an eye. You hear what that guy just called me? Roy Rogers' horse. He called me Trigger." Having absorbed the initial blow quite well, Gregory next reclaimed command of the audience with more of his predetermined countermaterial for racist hecklers:

> You know, my contract reads that every time I hear that word, I get fifty dollars more a night. I'm only making ten dollars a night, and I'd like to put the owner out of business. Will everybody in the room please stand up and yell nigger?[36]

No record company or newspaper would have published material featuring use of the word "nigger," one of the most inciting terms in American history. Therefore, it is nearly impossible to verify and reconstruct the atmosphere and exchanges of the harsher racist heckling Gregory experienced beyond his own recollections. The historical record does reflect, however, Gregory's professional fortunes in the early 1960s. He gained greater notoriety as a comedian, and he made his television debut in an ABC documentary about the race situation in the North. The special program featuring Gregory served as a "pertinent and hard-hitting reminder that racial prejudice exists in many ways and many places outside the South."[37]

The new year brought an amazing opportunity. Hugh Hefner, head of the *Playboy Magazine* enterprise, gave Gregory his big break when he booked him as a fill-in at the Playboy Club in Chicago in 1961. After arriving, Gregory was informed that the stage manager had decided it was best to postpone his debut because a group of southern white men in town for a frozen food convention had rented out the room where he was scheduled to perform. He refused to be turned away, and he instead gambled on his ability to be funny before a potentially hostile crowd. Gregory's risk paid off nicely. "The audience, Chicagoans, Northerners and Southerners, laughed, clapped and begged for more," Hefner recalled.[38] Gregory shined in delivering his brand of comedy and social criticism before an all-white crowd on the big stage. Hefner offered him a regular job at a salary of fifty dollars per night.[39]

Dexter Gordon has argued that African American humor is "always making visible the invisible while masking its own anger and rage."[40] The characterization is appropriate for Gregory's act, especially when he entertained an audience filled with people whose homes he likely would not have been allowed to enter because of his skin color. Gregory launched one of his most important attacks against racism in America using a subtle tool of cultural protest. He immediately sought to defuse any racial tension: "Good evening, ladies and gentlemen, I understand there are a good many Southerners in the room tonight. I know the South very well. I spent twenty years there one night."[41] Gregory later entertained his audience with a bit about a trip he had recently taken to the South:

> I sit down, a blonde waitress walked over to me. I say: *I'd like two cheeseburgers.*
>
> She say: *We don't serve colored people down here.*
>
> I say: *I don't eat colored people nowhere!*
>
> About that time, the three brothers walked in, and if you've ever been to Mississippi, you know what three brothers I'm talking about—Klu, Kluck, and Klan. The big one walked up and kicked my chair.
>
> He say: *Boy, you know damn well you can't eat in here.*

I say: *Just for that, bring me a whole fried chicken.*

He say: *Boy, you can't eat that chicken in here, and what-EVER you do to that chicken in here, we gonna do to you.*

I say: *For a dollar and a quarter? I'm with integration, but don't rush it!*

Twenty minutes later the waitress brought the chicken out, put it down in front of me. I was putting salt and pepper on it. He walked back up again and say: *Boy, by golly we done already told you. What-EVER you do to that chicken down here, we gonna do to you.*

I was feeling so good, I told him: *Y'all line up.* I kissed it.[42]

Newsweek reported that as soon as Gregory was booked at the Playboy Club, "Jim Crow was dead in the joke world."[43] Considering that he was not threatened or harmed beyond some early heckling, it is clear that Gregory challenged American racism before an all-white audience and *won*. No law, resolution, or policy was enacted following his gig, but the night was important nonetheless. Joseph Mancini later proclaimed Gregory "the first Negro comic to succeed in sophisticated cabarets."[44] Gregory was the first African American to establish stand-up comedy performed before predominantly white audiences as a method of protest against segregation and Jim Crow.

The degree to which Gregory's material centered on America's race problem is difficult to determine. Given the differences in location, audience, and current events, no two shows were the same. Time appears to have been a significant factor as well. More than a year after his debut at the Playboy Club, an article by Dave Hepburn in the *New York Amsterdam News* assessed Gregory's range of topics beyond racial matters:

> The most outstanding thing about Dick Gregory is, contrary to what you have heard, he is not a "Negro" comic. He is a Negro, but his material is general. His social comment is about all phases of our society, from W. Alton Jones' death on a plane to the price of meat.

He further explained that Gregory "employed more racial jokes at the beginning of his career, but now he has leveled off and broadened his scope, with success." Gregory, too, assessed his balance between racial and nonracial jokes. He stated that "jokes on integration and the racial problem are only fifteen percent of my nightly material."[45] While it is clear that Gregory staked an identity in mainstream America as an intelligent African American comedian with biting yet humorous material centered on racial issues, it is also apparent that his act was engaging on other levels. His presentation of racial *and* nonracial material was shockingly new to white America.

Whenever Gregory told racial jokes to predominantly white audiences, it was purposeful. In October 1961, an entertainment trade journal concluded that Gregory's racial material was "carefully measured so that, while it might bruise some white skins, it wouldn't draw blood."[46] Gregory carved out his own form of direct action that should be interpreted as a method of resistance against the Jim Crow racial order. He transformed the comic stage into a platform for protest and leadership in the struggle for African American freedom and ushered in a new cultural politics in the arena of comedy. Gregory's attitude in performing before predominantly white audiences was, "We're all aware of what's going on here, aren't we, baby?"[47] He did not envision success for an African American comedian who avoided the matter of race. But he could not have been more wrong, as a young, charismatic guy from Philadelphia who became the "fresh prince" of African American comedy soon proved.

Cosby's path to stardom began nearly a year after Gregory's breakout performance at the Playboy Club in January 1961. He needed funds to support himself as a twenty-four-year-old college student, and he accepted a bartending job making five dollars a week at a spot called the Cellar. Maintaining a light atmosphere for customers was a part of Cosby's role. He took ownership of the additional duty by developing jokes longer than typical one-liners. He used a table to create the semblance of a stage, but his height prevented him from standing erect. The creative Cosby solved the dilemma by placing a chair on the table and entertaining customers from his seat. His career in stand-up actually began by sitting down.

The Underground, an entertainment establishment located in the same building as the Cellar, gave Cosby more of an opportunity to showcase his comedic skills. He gained experience telling his jokes primarily to integrated crowds of college students, and he soon began to try his luck at any Philadelphia venue that would give him an opportunity. "I went to a beatnik dive—you know the kind—full of ugly Negro girls and ugly white men—sort of a Lonelyhearts integration. But they laughed," Cosby remembered.[48] He had developed a reputation as a "rather loquacious dispenser of spirits, regaling the customers with his odd brand of humor."[49] Cosby's schedule was taxing. He was a full-time student in the fall of 1961, and his participation in football, basketball, and track at Temple further reduced his amount of free time. He spent his days going back and forth between the classroom, athletic arenas, and nightclubs.

Cosby connected with an agent within his first several months of performing. Herb Gart, a fellow undergraduate student at Temple who was white, had managed a few friends who were folk singers. He was "keenly ambitious about show business and very smart." Gart had seen Cosby work as an emcee, and he quickly entered into a partnership with his Temple classmate. He appreciated Cosby's humor:

> One of my favorite moments with Bill was when we were sitting in a breakfast-restaurant with his niece, who had come in from Harrisburg. She was wide-eyed, she said, "Oh, Philadelphia! It's so exciting!" And Cos paused, and muttered, "You poor child." It was a great comment on Philly.[50]

In early 1962, Gart and Cosby learned about a search for new talent at Gaslight Café, a popular coffeehouse in New York City. Management at the Greenwich Village establishment was scouting performers for shows that would be held in the summer. The pair decided to give it a shot. "We went up there for him to audition," Gart remembered. "He did a guest set, and of course got the gig." Cosby considered it his first big-time opportunity. He was thrilled by the prospect of performing on a bigger stage than the Philadelphia clubs he had played previously. "Cosby could hardly wait for the semester to end," Gart recalled. "Summer in New York City, playing a real New York club!" His audience at the Gaslight consisted mainly of bohemian youths and college students. He performed as many as six sets on some evenings, and he slept in a room above the business. The inconveniences were worth bearing in his quest to become a "seasoned performer in front of a sophisticated audience," a prerequisite to more lucrative bookings.[51]

Paul Gardner, a *New York Times* journalist, covered Cosby's act. He introduced the young comedian to readers with a subheading that summarized his material—"Philadelphia Negro Aims His Barbs at Race Relations."[52] Cosby's early comedy was indeed peppered with as many racial jokes as Gregory's. By 1962, many whites were saying, "Bring on more comedians like Gregory," and Cosby met the demand: "I used to live in a nice neighborhood," he would share. "Then two white families moved in."[53] Cosby developed more humorous material centered on America's race problem. He portrayed himself as the nation's first African American president in one of his bits: "Yeh, baby, everything's fine, except a lot of 'for sale' signs are going up on this block." One of the quips he used for white audience members who appeared not to enjoy his show was, "You better laugh. I've got a club that's the opposite of the Klu Klux Klan."[54]

Cosby's early career suggested he was headed for success as a carbon copy of Gregory. "I was telling racial jokes then," he explained. "You know, the biting, witty kind about the Negro's role in America. But pretty soon critics regarded me as a sort of hip Nipsey Russell or Philadelphia Dick Gregory." Even Cosby failed to identify any significant difference between him and Gregory, who was a wealthy celebrity by the summer of 1962. "Some people call me 'the Philadelphia Dick Gregory,'" he joked, "but that's silly. I'm taller—and better looking."[55] At that time, in any case, they were the same type of comedian.

Cosby's shift began that summer. It was aided by his manager, who gave him comedy material to listen to in his room. One of the performers' albums Cosby heard was Lord Buckley, a comedic entertainer who "often recited Biblical stories" in a rhythmical jargon commonly referred to as "hip."[56] Buckley's classic rendition of "Jonah and the Whale" almost certainly provided Cosby with the inspiration to develop his "Noah" routines. Cosby's humorous retelling of the exchanges between Noah and God became wildly popular, and it helped catapult him to mainstream success. Cosby also studied comedians whose live performances he caught while in New York City. He had a deep appreciation of Lenny Bruce's ability to engage audiences with the characters he created onstage, and he "would try to free-form like Lenny and offer up some anecdotes."[57] Cosby had always tried new styles as he worked to develop a unique act. In Philadelphia, he had occasionally adopted Mort Sahl's shtick of walking onstage with a folded newspaper beneath his arm. His star continued to rise in the summer of 1962 despite his ongoing search for a professional identity. In Chicago, where Gregory had already appeared on white America's radar, Cosby was noted for his "wit and know-how which is seldom experienced at the age of 24."[58]

"I found that to be a success," stated Cosby, "I'd have to jump over Dick Gregory. I had the shadow of Gregory in everything I did." He decided to shed the label of "Negro comedian" by dropping his race jokes. Cosby and his new manager, Roy Silver, a twenty-nine-year-old white male, invested a significant amount of planning in the effort. Both knew he was better as "a comedian in the Twain mold, observing all aspects of human nature, a comedian who just happened to be black."[59] Humor that allowed him to showcase his excellent timing and characters would be his ticket. Cosby became a specialist at entertaining audiences with the type of humor evident in his Noah routines:

> Of course, Noah had a heck of a job, really. He had to go out and collect all of the animals in the world by twos. Two mosquitoes . . . And, he had to keep telling the rabbits, *Only two, only two, only two.* So we find Noah pulling up the last two animals, two hippos, and he's really in a hurry to get them up because he's afraid that the Lord's gonna call him and ask him to do something else. And his nerves are shot. This is one heck of a job for a man 600 years old.
>
> So we find him pulling up the last two hippos, and, of course, the Lord does call him there.
>
> [Noah]: Come on, fat hippos. Hurry up! Come on, will ya please?
>
> [God]: Noah.
>
> [Noah]: What?! What do you want?
>
> [God]: Gotta take one of those hippos out and bring in another one.
>
> [Noah]: What for?
>
> [God]: 'Cause you got two males down there, and you need to bring in a female.
>
> [Noah]: I'm not bringing nothing in. You change one of 'em.

[God]: Come on, you know I don't work like that.

[Noah]: Well I'm sick and tired of this. I've had enough of this stuff. I've been working all day. I've been working hard for days and days. I'm sick and tired of this!

[God]: Noah?

[Noah]: Yeah.

[God]: How long can you tread water?[60]

Developing and maintaining this type of nonracial comedy had its difficulties. Cosby resorted to using racial jokes on the nights his tall tales seemed unsatisfying to his audience. Silver grew livid when Cosby diverted from their plan, and the two often squared off violently once Cosby exited the stage. Cosby remembered the aftermath of the encounters: "Next morning, after we'd both cooled off a little, we'd get together and maybe develop another minute or two of material. It would be painful and hard."[61] Few outside the entertainment industry may understand the serious business of being a comedian. The pressure to capture the attention of many different people and focus it on a single idea that the comedian has deemed funny is enormous. Some comedians keep a pen and pad to record the slightest funny thought that might occur between shows, while running errands, or even in the middle of an overnight dream. The simplest observation can be developed into a valuable, routine-saving anecdote in the high-stakes business of comedy. After all, telling one or two jokes that fall flat early in a set often means losing the audience with no chance of winning them back. Yet the comedian's contract and reputation mandate that he or she continue to try! The bad nights can make just fifteen minutes feel like an eternity. Perhaps Cosby's manager did not comprehend the frustration that caused him to fall back on the racial jokes when audiences seemed unreceptive to his newer material.

Despite its challenges, the summer in New York proved productive for Cosby. He found his onstage identity. No more race jokes. He would stake his success in the business by defining himself as the anti–Dick Gregory. "I feel that I have no right to speak for all Negroes," Cosby said. He would still make efforts to speak out against white supremacy, but he would do it "as an American, not as an entertainer."[62] The strategy paid immediate dividends. After returning to Philadelphia to begin the fall semester of his sophomore year, Cosby was invited back to New York City in the spring of 1963. "Bill Cosby is one of America's up-and-coming young Negro comics," one writer noted. "However, unlike the others, Bill doesn't tell race jokes."[63]

Cosby's decision to drop the race jokes created a permanent divide between him and Gregory. It gave the appearance of two African American comedians with opposing styles and politics, although no two performers could have been more similar prior to the moment he crafted a new identity. Cosby may actually have been motivated to drop the race jokes in an attempt to become more *like* Gregory than different from him. Dave Hepburn's lengthy article, titled "Dick Gregory's Rags-to-Riches Break Good for Half a Million," was printed in New York City's African American newspaper, the *Amsterdam News*, in June 1962, the same time that Cosby was performing at the Gaslight.[64] Hepburn's article gave considerable attention to Gregory's evolution into a comedian whose jokes were not focused primarily on race. It is possible that the report of Gregory's astounding success as a comedian who had eclipsed the racial tag—and stood to make $500,000 that year—influenced Cosby's decision to drop his race jokes. Although the story may not have been an entirely accurate presentation of Gregory's material, Cosby elected to situate himself at the silent end of the spectrum of entertainers who used their platforms to speak out against racism.

Both Gregory and Cosby rose to fame in a changing America. White America had recently begun to enjoy African American entertainment beyond those performances that reinforced negative stereotypes. The shift was already noticeable in the music industry. Brian Ward's study of the crossover sales of African American music from 1954 to 1963 suggests that the Civil Rights Movement gained momentum from the relationship between liberal white youth and African American artists.[65] Although R&B music was also met with resistance from white America, an emerging biracial music culture helped encourage African American artists to politicize their lyrics. Changes in America's social landscape similarly aided the meteoric rise of Gregory and Cosby. The explanation of Gregory's success offered by columnist Hilda See—"'Tis timely, pals, timely in these days of sit-ins and the like in Dixie"—reflected the nation's evolving society, although its intent appears to have been to undercut Gregory's unique talent and diligence.[66]

Gregory had indeed emerged as an African American comedian with commentary on political and social matters at a time when resistance to racism was understood and encouraged by more whites than ever before. The long Civil Rights Movement that intensified after World War II had begun to attract greater cross-racial support and cooperation. Key events, such as large-scale school desegregation mandated by the *Brown v. Board of Education of Topeka, Kansas* case in 1954, the Montgomery Bus Boycott in 1955, and the student sit-ins in 1960, helped prepare white America for the rise of an African American comedian like Gregory, who forged his own attack on segregation and Jim Crow. His material may not have gained such popularity ten years prior, but by the early 1960s, many whites were clamoring for more of his satire that positioned him as a "drum major for justice" in the cultural arena. Gregory enabled "colored and white to laugh together about their mutually discomforting problems for the first time in a half century."[67] He became the most sought-after and highest-paid African American stand-up comedian of the early 1960s because his act was packed with style, substance, and sting.

Most whites celebrated Gregory's success in the spotlight in 1961 and 1962. Comedian Bob Hope praised his breakout performance at the Playboy Club. "You're terrific," he told Gregory.[68] Arthur Gelb lauded him as "the only member of his race thus far to join with and hold his own in the ranks of the bright, young, intellectually oriented, wittily topical, stand-up comics."[69] The assessment would hold true until Cosby joined him in 1963. While Hugh Hefner had paid Gregory a salary of $250 a week at the beginning of 1961, his fee jumped to nearly $2,500 a week by the spring. *The Jack Paar Show*, a popular late-night talk program, offered the comedian access to the American mainstream. During his first live television performance, he explained to the host, "I'm glad I voted for Kennedy. I hear he's gonna air-condition the cotton fields."[70] One observer commented on the importance of television for Gregory and other African American comedians who followed his new politics of representation in comedy: "But for television the new crop would not be receiving the recognition that is coming their way."[71] The appearance on the *Paar* show maximized Gregory's visibility, and it helped him earn a $25,000 advance from Colpix Records for two comedy albums. The first, *In Living Black & White*, became a top-50 best seller.[72]

Journalist Gilbert Millstein described Gregory for his readers who may not have seen his act. Gregory was dark and slender but "powerfully put together." Millstein added that Gregory had "round, innocent eyes, a round, ingenuous face, mouth and voice, and a small, crescent-shaped mustache. Nothing in his appearance or delivery is at all in consonance with what he says." Gregory's physical appearance was especially appealing to a white female audience member one evening. "My God," she interrupted his routine and spoke, "you're good looking. I sure would like to love you." Gregory navigated the tense moment by first asking the woman her nationality, which was Hungarian. He next eased the discomfort in the room with his quick wit: "Take two more drinks, and you'll say you're colored, run up here and kiss me and we'll both leave town in a hurry."[73] Even during such random interactions with white audience members, Gregory demonstrated the new style of his humor by "distill[ing] the poignancy of racial conflict into wise and wry laughter."[74] Whites raved over Gregory's act in large part because his material was socially relevant as well as entertaining.

Praise and recognition for Gregory poured in from a variety of sources. He won an Owl Award from *Show Business Illustrated* as "Comedian of the Year" in 1961.[75] The women's division of the American Jewish Congress recognized Gregory in 1962 for his "contributions of humor and wit in the fight against bigotry and bias" and honored him at a luncheon where he was presented an original oil painting from the Louise Waterman Wise Youth Center in Jerusalem.[76] Gregory noted the irony of racism's role in his success: "Where else but in America do I have to ride in the back of the bus, eat in second-class restaurants, live in third-rate apartments—and get $5,000 per week for talking about it!"[77] Even the US Congress recognized Gregory as a cultural icon and civil rights champion. A particular quip reverberated in Washington, DC: "Discrimination exists in the North, too; only when Northerners want to get rid of all Negroes in a certain area, they have a slum clearance." Based on this strike against racial oppression—delivered through the medium of stand-up comedy—Gregory was asked to testify before a Senate subcommittee hearing on Involuntary Relocation of the Aged.[78]

The reaction to Gregory from other African American comedians and performers was mixed. Cosby was thankful that Gregory created inroads that afforded him bookings in New York City in 1962 that would not have been possible otherwise. Moms Mabley, Nipsey Russell, and Slappy White were also booked at the Playboy Club in Chicago following Gregory's incredibly successful run. Russell joined Timmie Rogers in becoming a frequent guest on the *Jack Paar Show* following Gregory's appearance—a major boost to both of their careers. Redd Foxx, a veteran comedian whose "blue" material prohibited his act from scoring with mainstream America, summarized Gregory's major accomplishment: "Greg opened the door," he said.[79] Yet Foxx was bitter about Gregory's unprecedented appeal and creative license with white America. During a previous failed audition to appear on the *Ed Sullivan Show*, Foxx recalled being warned to "stay off the South, white women, the Congo and the President." He viewed Gregory as undeserving, in part, because his own talent and longevity had been overlooked. Russell, meanwhile, voiced his resentment of the expectations Gregory established:

> *Now* the bookers tell us we *can* do social satire. *Now*, I'm being courted to do records other than party albums. But they're still categorizing me as a *Negro* comedian. Damn it, I want to make it as a comedian, period. But the way things are going now, every time we come on the floor we'll be expected to say something funny about a lynching.[80]

African American newspapers followed Gregory's act closely. They were not as immediate as the white press in validating his talent. Al Monroe questioned Gregory's detachment from the previous vein of African American comedic performers: "To say that Richard Gregory is of that old school is not exactly true.—However it is just as doubtful that his comedy can be removed from the classification entirely." Monroe charged that Gregory's material often matched the prior group of African American comedic performers whose jokes were laced with "references to color of one's skin, plight of the Negro in Dixieland; the texture of hair based on interracial difference and the character of females (including the comedian's wife)."[81] Jesse H. Walker captured the more common criticism directed at Gregory in African American circles: "A lot of his material, seemingly new to the Paar audience wasn't new to us; in fact, we've heard a lot of it in Negro homes, and said more for ironic effect than humor."[82]

The concern that Gregory had commodified jokes previously shared among African Americans was legitimate. He introduced humor that ridiculed segregation and Jim Crow to many thousands of whites, who enjoyed the new strain of comedy. Many African Americans, however, resented how whites showered Gregory with fame and fortune based on material that was not necessarily his own. The dilemma exposed the dichotomy between African American private and public humor. Criticizing America's racist society with entertaining satire was indeed nothing new in African American homes, churches, and other segregated spaces. The humor exchanged in these locations was considered private because it was enjoyed in the absence of whites. The jokes were biting and often wildly hilarious, and they were considered the intellectual property of the entire race, especially because whites were usually cast as the butt of the jokes. Gregory violated an unwritten code by adapting this material for use in the public sphere—environments that included whites, such as the Playboy Club in Chicago and Blue Angel in New York City. No prior African American comedian had introduced the racial material from African American private spaces to the mainstream. Gregory was confident enough to interact with white audiences and deliver biting social criticism along racial lines that many other African American performers were unwilling or unable to voice in the public sphere.

Cosby's decision to drop his race jokes in the summer of 1962 freed him from the discussion. Still in his infancy compared to Gregory, the only recorded concern in the white press about his act was that "his output is thus far limited."[83] The more forward-looking review of his act in an African American newspaper suggested "a new star is being born."[84] Both Gregory and Cosby had come to the stage in the early 1960s with fierce determination and unmistakable talent. Their paths had been eerily similar, but the divergence had begun. In 1962, Cosby did not earn even a tenth of Gregory's income. However, his tales would soon become too tall for Gregory's satire to match.

Chapter 3

All of the Lights

In the mid-1960s, Gregory and Cosby made difficult choices that impacted their career trajectories. The long Civil Rights Movement had grown increasingly present in the cultural arena, and African American entertainment celebrities, such as Muhammad Ali and Harry Belafonte, had accepted the challenge to apply their notoriety toward advancing the struggle for freedom. Gregory and Cosby differed from one another in their responses to the call for activism. The former marched steadfastly into a leadership role in the Civil Rights Movement despite the risks to his lucrative career. He discussed his unthinking decision in a 2002 interview with Camille Cosby (Bill Cosby's wife) as part of the National Visionary Leaders Project:

> I had something to lose—I didn't know it. Let me just set the record straight. If you could feel your hair grow, you'd probably go crazy. You don't feel it grow. And so, it's the same way when I made it [as an entertainer]. I went from here to here, and no one said, "This is what it's going to be like, and here's the chances." So, nobody sat with me and said, "If you get involved [in the movement], your income is this, it's gonna go to this, if you get involved." Nobody. Hell, I didn't have an option. It was moving so fast. It's just, I liked what I felt, and if that meant death—You know, something's wrong with someone who is willing to commit their life, but then worry about their income.[1]

Cosby, alternatively, privileged his finances over leadership in the movement. He aimed to increase his earnings exponentially by breaking into television and film, which required greater mainstream appeal than that typically afforded to fiery African American civil rights activists. Applying his celebrity status toward direct action campaigns ran counter to Cosby's motivation to become wealthy. "I entered show business to make money, not to lead a march," he said in a 1965 interview. "Gregory's motives are genuine. He believes in freedom, he believes in the movement, he'll go anywhere to do a benefit." Cosby continued by explaining that instead of joining the front lines, he would "rather send a thousand dollars to the Deacons [for Defense]."[2] Lance Hill's reconstruction of the activities of this bold self-defense organization formed in Louisiana reveals that it kept incredibly poor financial records, so it may be impossible to determine if Cosby's remark was more than banter.[3] He had enjoyed rapid growth with respect to career opportunities and finances in just two years as a professional stand-up comedian, and he was by all means determined to maintain his popularity with mainstream America by continuing his "anti–Dick Gregory" approach to entertainment and civil rights.

Gregory released his fourth album, *My Brother's Keeper*, in 1963. It was a political statement rather than a comedy project. Gregory used his personal funds to produce and distribute the album, which centered on racial inequality and other social injustices. All of the profits were redirected to aid the struggle for freedom in one of the most racially charged locations in the nation—Mississippi. Gregory had become concerned about racial oppression in the state after a visitor at a Chicago comedy club asked him to endorse a fund-raising letter in support of African Americans in the Mississippi Delta facing "starvation conditions."[4] County officials in Sunflower and Leflore Counties had cut off the federal food supply of approximately 20,000 impoverished African American residents. Activists charged that withdrawal from the U.S. food surplus distribution program was punishment for increased voter registration. Aubrey Bell, attorney for the Leflore County Board of Supervisors, told two federal civil rights investigators the accusation was a "damn lie." He further explained that white Mississippians resented "Negroes being brought to the Clerk's Office by outside racial agitators and that racial conditions in Mississippi had always been harmonious until the Federal Government and outside agitators started sticking their noses into the State's business."[5] Bell maintained the position of the white power structure in Sunflower and Leflore Counties—the food program had been discontinued because the $37,000 cost of storing and distributing the food could not be afforded.[6]

Contrary to Bell's claim of harmonious racial conditions, relations between African Americans and whites in Mississippi had long been contentious. John Dittmer's *Local People: The Struggle for Civil Rights in Mississippi* reconstructs the activities of thousands of post–World War II African Americans who put their lives on the line battling white supremacy in the face of seemingly insurmountable odds. Voting discrimination and intimidation tactics were the most common frustrations, which Dittmer evidences with a document submitted to Congress in 1946—nearly two decades before the Voting Rights Act of 1965 was passed. "On September 19," he writes, "fifty Mississippians (including several whites) filed a complaint with the U.S. Senate Committee to Investigate Campaigning Expenditures, claiming that [Senator Theodore] Bilbo had subjected blacks to a 'reign of terror' during [his] campaign and urging the full Senate to impeach Bilbo and remove him from office."[7] The decision by Mississippi state officials to withdraw from the food surplus program was among a lengthy record of aggressive tactics designed to perpetuate African American disenfranchisement.

My Brother's Keeper was a large part of the resistance effort Gregory led on behalf of oppressed African Americans in the Mississippi Delta. Only 37,000 copies were sold, and each unit was priced at $1.60. The manufacturing cost of each album was $0.60, and Gregory planned to send the entire $37,000 profit from the sale of the 37,000 units to the Leflore County Board of Supervisors so they could "continue the distribution of surplus food to those in need, both black and white." The album was recorded live before a predominantly white audience of 1,000 people on the campus of San Diego State College. It began after Gregory entertained the crowd with a comedy set, and it included discussion of his views on "the Negro, race relations, integration, the Black Muslims, and the very nature of man himself." Gregory was occasionally humorous on the record, but his anger, resentment, and frustration with the race problem in America were evident. He spent a significant amount of time discussing racial oppression in Mississippi. He mentioned the state's governor, Ross Barnett, while sharing his thoughts on the "problem" posed by people of African descent in American society:

> Wherever you have racial tension, you have people that can't think. A Negro problem? There's no Negro problem in America.

> Show me a Negro problem in America, and I'll show you dumb white leadership—Governor Barnett, [and] any incident you find. We (African Americans) don't control anything. So we can't have a problem.[8]

When asked to describe the difference between a northern and southern liberal, Gregory delivered a reply consistent with his brand of satire:

> I actually don't really see too much difference in the two of them. Most of the liberals say, *What can we give you tomorrow?* The people that's hung up in this minority struggle are saying, *Give it to me today.* The constitution of this great country mentions nothing about tomorrow. It says today, which is what more people are beginning to wake up to today. The Northern liberal and the Southern liberal, to me, represent the third man in a fist fight.

Gregory volunteered his thoughts on religion during the approximately half-hour question and answer session. His comments elicited a round of nervous laughter:

> Religion has failed us. And when I say religion has failed us, I mean exactly, religion has failed us. I can take you back to Chicago Sunday morning, and I can take you into twenty churches that they wouldn't let me in. But few taverns [would let me in]. Kinda makes you wonder which one of those buildings should the cross be on.[9]

My Brother's Keeper went on sale the week of March 16, 1963. The NAACP took the task of selling 10,000 copies.[10] Proceeds from album sales were enough to cover the cost of storing and distributing food supplies in Sunflower and Leflore Counties, although newspapers reported conflicting information regarding the allocation of the funds. An article published on March 27 quoted Gregory as saying, "County officials said it would take $37,000 to handle the food, so that's why I waxed the album. I'm calling their bluff."[11] However, on March 30, the *New York Amsterdam News* reported that proceeds from Gregory's album would be used to "buy staple products."[12] The latter corresponds with a "Food for Freedom Drive" Gregory had announced on January 31, 1963, along with the Chicago Area Friends of the Student Nonviolent Coordinating Committee (SNCC). Gregory later explained why the money raised from the sale of *My Brother's Keeper* was not needed for either purpose: "The record went over big. The NAACP alone took 10,000 copies to sell. But now the federal government has taken over the distribution costs and the people are getting their surplus rations again." He detailed how his new plan for the album's $37,000 profit matched one of his ongoing initiatives to rehabilitate misguided youth: "I'm going to round up about 50 young gang leaders all over the country and carry them down to Hawaii. And they can thank the white officials of Leflore (Greenwood) County, Miss., for the $37,000 I'm going to spend on them."[13] Gregory truly cared more about improving conditions for the disfranchised than about money. While no record exists of him conducting a retreat in Hawaii with young gang members, sizeable gifts like his initial and revised pledge of proceeds from *My Brother's Keeper* set Gregory apart from his contemporaries.

Luvaghn Brown, a SNCC field secretary in Jackson, Mississippi, discussed the Food for Freedom Drive at a news conference he and Gregory held before the federal government agreed to cover the costs of its food surplus program in Sunflower and Leflore Counties. Brown explained that the food drive was necessary because "most of the Negroes are employed in cotton harvesting but must rely on federal surpluses to feed them during the winter months when they are unemployed."[14] His analysis was accurate. Dittmer's research indicates that "nearly two-thirds of the black male labor force engaged in some form of agriculture-related activity."[15] SNCC's involvement was linked to its perception among many white Mississippians as "outside racial agitators."[16] The organization had conducted a voter registration campaign in Sunflower and Leflore Counties since May of the previous year, and its leadership chose not to abandon those whom the organization had sought to empower politically. While their voter registration efforts were successful—fewer than 100 of the nearly 70,000 African Americans in the counties had registered to vote before their arrival—they were not without consequence, as white county officials likely cut off the federal food supply because of the increase in political activism that SNCC operatives helped engineer.[17]

The Food for Freedom Drive spearheaded by Gregory and co-sponsored by SNCC was ambitious. During its first phase, 20,000 pounds of food were to be delivered to the Mississippi Delta from February 1–10, 1963. Churches, clubs, organizations, and prominent Chicagoans were tapped to donate money and "urgently needed" staples, such as flour, cornmeal, rice, sugar, powdered milk, cereals, dried beans, cooking fats, and canned foods.[18] Organizers set up more than thirty-five drop-off points in the Chicago area, and the *Defender* reported the response as being "so generous . . . that the original estimate has been upped to 50,000 pounds."[19] The plan was to airlift the food to Greenville, Mississippi, located in the heart of the Mississippi Delta, where it would then be distributed by the Council of Federated Organizations. Gregory generated more publicity for the operation by escorting the first shipment of approximately 14,000 pounds of food down south. His plane stopped in Memphis, where he went on record as saying, "Mississippi is part of the United States, you know. They don't know it yet, but they will pretty soon."[20]

The picture of Gregory leading a caravan of trucks from Memphis to Greenville represents an important part of his personal attack against Jim Crow in the Mississippi Delta, but his efforts produced far greater results than the simple imagery of resistance. Cooperation, support, and momentum spread widely. Martin Luther King Jr. joined the second phase of the Food for Freedom Drive with a nationwide appeal: "I'm calling on supporters North, South, East and West to gather staple goods in their communities through their churches to be sent to the Council of Federated Organizations at Clarksdale, Mississippi."[21] By mid-February, an additional 30,000 pounds of food were scheduled for delivery from Chicago to Sunflower and Leflore Counties. The *Defender* reported that participation transcended the boundaries of age, race, and faith:

> Hundreds of high school and university students participated in the campaign. White, Negro, Jewish, Catholic, Protestant; churches, snygagogues [sic], block clubs, organizations and bowling lanes all joined in the campaign when the need was spotlighted by comic Dick Gregory and the committee.

One white restaurant owner donated "100 pounds each of rice, sugar, flour, barley, cornmeal, and other staples."[22] This generous contribution to assist African Americans in Mississippi highlights Gregory's unique position as a comedian-activist with access to mainstream America. He joined a short list of entertainers, such as Muhammad Ali, Harry Belafonte, and Jackie Robinson, in actively transforming his "celebrity capital" into appropriate resources for use in the struggle for African American freedom.

Fred Ross, a white welfare commissioner in Mississippi, criticized Gregory's activism in the Delta. He called Gregory's involvement with the Food for Freedom Drive a "cheap publicity stunt" and voiced concerns about its long-term ramifications: "People of good will in this state who have demonstrated their desire to minister to the needy, rather than the greedy, may find it impossible to do so in the future." Ross warned that state officials might decide against taxing its citizens to fund future food distribution programs and instead leave the responsibility in the hands of "Dick Gregory and his Chicago cohorts."[23] Other white state officials were equally critical of Gregory. Records of the Mississippi State Sovereignty Commission, a state-funded anti–civil rights agency that existed from 1956 to 1977, referred to him as a "Negro clown" who joined other outside racial agitators in stirring up trouble.[24] Thousands of white Mississippians likely shared the scorn for Gregory and the Food for Freedom Drive. In this unique racial hotbed, common knowledge dictated that "uppity Negroes" who defied hierarchical norms placed themselves at risk of backlash from white supremacists.

Gregory's activities in the state of Mississippi demonstrate his successful merging of culture and politics. His willingness to join the front lines in one of the most dangerous locales in the nation for African American activists provides clear evidence that his stage persona was more than a shtick. Mississippi was known for its unchecked violence that placed enormous fear in the minds of its African American residents day after day. Dittmer's analysis suggests that African American ministers and middle-class professionals carried the banner of freedom in other southern states but were often forced into observer roles in Mississippi by personal and economic threats very likely to be carried out by violent white mobs and racist white professionals. Gregory must have been aware that a white mob in the Mississippi Delta had kidnapped, beaten, and murdered thirteen-year-old Emmett Till in 1955 for whistling at a white woman. And he was certainly aware of the threats and intimidation endured by his friend Medgar Evers, a native Mississippian and the state's first NAACP field secretary. When Evers was shot and killed by a white supremacist a few months after Gregory escorted a caravan of trucks into Greenville, Gregory did not retreat. He continued to risk his life and livelihood by antagonizing white Mississippians who sought to protect the social order of "white over black." Gregory's autobiography reflects his dual worries about returning to lead a march in Greenwood, Mississippi, shortly after the Food for Freedom Drive:

> If Whitey down South doesn't kill me in Greenwood, then Whitey up North will kill me in show business. Everybody I talked to but Lil told me not to go. It would ruin me as a

comic. Nobody's going to come to laugh at an entertainer who goes marching and demonstrating and getting himself arrested.[25]

Other activists may have elected to avoid joining the struggle in the Mississippi Delta because of its volatile racial climate. The sovereignty commission collected detailed information about rallies and meetings in which Gregory participated during his stay in Greenwood, and it noted the absence of other invitees: "Rumors were circulating to the effect that Jackie Robinson and Rev. Martin Luther King would be present, but they failed to show."[26] Gregory, Robinson, and King had received strong criticism in 1961 from the *Jackson Daily News*, a white newspaper in Jackson, Mississippi, for being among the "loudest advocates for Negroes and whites to join Freedom Rides, but who haven't been on the buses themselves." The press leveled an especially serious charge against King, whom it accused of taking in large sums of money while "Cadillacking about the country making speeches and taking bows in the relative and or welcome safety of northern environments." The newspaper also noted the absence of Ralph Bunche, Sammy Davis, Jr., Cidney [sic] Poitier, and Harry Belafonte from the dangerous front lines in the South.[27]

Gregory's determined battle against injustice and inequality in the Mississippi Delta provided evidence of his genuine interest in contributing to the struggle for African American freedom. The Sovereignty Commission may never have questioned his sincerity, as a report filed on April 4, 1963, mentioned that "Gregory stated in his talk the night before that he was in Greenwood to stay until Negroes' freedom was obtained."[28] Upon his return North, Gregory remembered being uniquely bothered by questions and accusations about his work down south. He accepted that white editors in the North had likely twisted reports of his activism, but he grew quite disturbed by doubt expressed by fellow African Americans:

> But what scared me most was when Negroes asked me if it was true that I had gone down to Greenwood for publicity.
> And it dawned on me that anytime you help a Negro in America, even the Negroes will question your intentions. I could have quit show business and joined the Peace Corps and gone to Vietnam and no one, white or black, would have questioned why I did it. But to help Negroes . . .
> I was just beginning to realize what a long hard row it would be.[29]

Gregory spent most of 1963 in a tense battle against white supremacists in Mississippi. The *Defender* labeled the comedian a "one-man NAACP" based on his leadership of the Food for Freedom Drive and other direct action campaigns in the state.[30] Gregory played pivotal roles in the plights of James Meredith and Clyde Kennard, African American men in Mississippi whose suffering became known by many across the nation. In 1962, Meredith became the first African American admitted to the University of Mississippi, albeit with great controversy. Ross Barnett, governor of Mississippi, refused to protect Meredith as he attended his first day of classes amid an angry, vicious crowd of white segregationists, including students, on the university's campus. President John F. Kennedy dispatched the National Guard to Oxford, Mississippi, to ensure the peace. The Guard proved unsuccessful, as two people were killed during the frenzy the night before Meredith's first day of class. Meredith's integration of the institution is a historical event entrenched in the minds of African American Mississippians. Elders and elementary students alike celebrate the breakthrough as a pivotal battle in what some describe as a second Civil War.

Meredith's experiences at the University of Mississippi campus reflected the tense racial environment that characterized America during its civil rights era. One report indicated "there has been strong speculation that Meredith, whose entrance at the university at the start of the fall semester touched off bloody riots, will not return for the second semester because of continued harassment and some apparent problems with grades." Gregory inserted himself into this international news story by striking up a friendship with Meredith. The men never discussed life at the University of Mississippi, as Gregory thought it was more beneficial to offer Meredith an escape from his trying experiences at the previously all-white institution. Meredith accepted Gregory's invitation to visit Chicago during the Christmas break following his first semester of study. Shots were fired into the home of Meredith's parents during his absence, and Gregory noted the occasion as "the first reaction I have ever known him to display."[31]

Meredith's matriculation carried significance as a challenge to segregation and Jim Crow in one of its most important bases, and it was closely monitored by many across the nation. His eventual graduation was a major victory in the struggle for African American freedom, and Gregory was credited by the *Chicago Defender* for his involvement: "He won't admit it, but Dick Gregory had a lot to do with James Meredith's decision on whether or not to stay at the University of Mississippi. Dick acted like a midwife in getting Meredith's mind made up."[32] The serious, emotional affair did not escape Gregory's satire. He complimented Meredith's academic integrity by saying, "You can be sure he didn't get any help on his exams from the other kids at the school."[33]

Clyde Kennard, a native of Hattiesburg, Mississippi, faced circumstances of even greater severity following his agitation for equal access to higher education. He spent three years at the University of Chicago before returning home because of family matters. He sought to complete his education at nearby Mississippi Southern College, an all-white institution. Officials at the college shared news of Kennard's educational goals with the press, which caused unrest among local white segregationists and increased the level of danger for Kennard. Dr. W.D. McCain, president of Mississippi Southern, expressed publicly that "there are several things which can be done in connection with the application if it is filed."[34]

Kennard temporarily ended the controversy surrounding his possible enrollment by withdrawing his interest in attending the college. "Upon the advice of many competent people," he wrote to President McCain in January 1959, "I have decided that to insist on my right to enroll at Mississippi Southern College at this point, perhaps, would not be in the best interest of the general community."[35] Kennard's consideration of the larger community did not last long. Records of the Mississippi Sovereignty Commission include a memorandum sent to the governor notifying him of Kennard's request for an admissions application in September 1959. Zack Van Landingham, the agent responsible for the communication, revealed President McCain as his source.[36] The chain of communication provides a glimpse into one of the most well-established white power structures in the nation during the 1960s.

Kennard was denied admission to Mississippi Southern based on "deficiencies and irregularities" in his application. He was arrested on campus upon returning to his car and charged with reckless driving. Constables claimed to have witnessed Kennard's moving violations before he arrived on campus.[37] While waiting for Kennard to return to his car, the constables also claimed to have found five half-pints of whiskey—illegal in the county—under his front seat.[38] Kennard was fined, but his ordeal had only begun. He was soon convicted of buying $25 worth of stolen chicken feed, and he received a seven-year prison sentence. He was treated once for intestinal cancer while incarcerated, but he was denied follow-up attention after severe hemorrhaging occurred. John Howard Griffin, a white journalist who chronicled the experiences of African Americans in the South, detailed Kennard's desperate condition:

> To everyone's disbelief, the warden refused to allow Clyde Kinard [sic] to return to the hospital and he was kept on the sunup to sundown gang. He had to be helped up in the morning and had to be carried back and put on his bed. If the weather was bad and his clothes were wet, he had to stay in wet clothes overnight. When he began to collapse before noon, he would be carried back in and the rule was that he could not walk to the cafeteria and no one could bring him food. He came to the conclusion that he was being allowed to die, not only by cancer but by starvation.[39]

Elaine Kennard, Clyde's sister, contacted Gregory for assistance. Gregory devised a strategy to apply greater pressure to state officials by widely publicizing their inhumane treatment of a dying inmate. "I thought that if all the facts were dug up and printed in the newspapers," he remembered, "America would get Kennard out of jail."[40] Gregory spent "approximately $15,000" to cover researchers' costs to join him on a fact-finding mission in Mississippi. His team obtained Kennard's medical record and shared his condition with the nation. The *Defender* lauded the accomplishment: "Even with a subpoena, attorneys for the doomed man (Kennard) had been unable to obtain the medical record." Kennard had spent nearly two years in prison by the time Gregory learned of his tragic circumstances. Governor Ross Barnett ordered Kennard to be released just two months after intense agitation led by the celebrity activist. Gregory recalled a simple but key action that likely was linked to his strategy to widely publicize Kennard's plight: "A Chicago millionaire called business connections in Mississippi, and Kennard was released from jail."[41] But there was no happy ending. Gregory arranged for Kennard to be brought to Chicago, where he died in Billings Hospital on July 4, 1963.[42] Historian John Dittmer regarded the matter as "the saddest story of the whole movement."[43]

Gregory's satirical brand of humor may have changed because of his experiences in Mississippi. In September 1963, Milton Esterow of the *New York Times* suggested that the comedian's "integration material is even sharper and cuts deeper."[44] Esterow's article included material that conveyed the "punch" in Gregory's act:

> You know the definition of a Southern moderate? That's a cat who will lynch you from a low tree.
>
> A man from the Ku Klux Klan once threatened to burn our house down. But his sheet caught on fire. We threw water at him, but we missed. We went back and filled our buckets—with gasoline.[45]

Esterow's assertion is difficult to prove or disprove. Gregory's humor had always been viewed as piercing, particularly his racial material. A change in the way he was perceived is more evident. Gregory's contributions to the struggle for African American freedom, especially in the South, were highly publicized, and many began to recognize him as more than a funnyman. "When Dick Gregory first started his comic routine, not many people gave him credit for being the thinker he is," Dave Hepburn wrote in March 1963. Hepburn added that "Dick has shown a tendency to become more and more profound."[46] James Wechsler, a white columnist for the *New York Post*, offered a stronger assertion of Gregory's transformation into a key activist who transcended the label of entertainer:

> Gregory is still officially billed as a comedian. But he is perhaps the most serious threat to the segregationist system to emerge in recent years. For he has cruelly reduced it to absurdity; he has transformed the counsels of "moderation" into a burlesque show; he has the passion of James Baldwin, but his weapon is ridicule, and it is deadly.[47]

Gregory's bookings continued to earn him large sums. His income had ballooned well into the six-figure range by 1963. He sacrificed tens of thousands by canceling or refusing shows that conflicted with his participation in civil rights protests, and he donated tens of thousands more to those involved in the struggle. "Gregory said he had canceled all his nightclub engagements," the *New York Post* reported while the comedian was in Greenwood to lead a march.[48] "Whether it's deductible or not," a Chicago columnist stated, "comic Dick Gregory in his serious moments last year spent a total of $60,000 on racial causes."[49]

In April 1963, Gregory charged that the Queens Club in New York City fired him because he announced the donation of his $6,500 weekly salary to activists in Mississippi. "As far as his claim that we fired him because of the Mississippi business, that is an entirely falsified statement," the club's spokesman responded. Management claimed to have fired Gregory because he showed up an hour late to perform. "I've been going on at 11:30 since I started there and all of a sudden I'm told I was supposed to be there at 10:30," Gregory said. The engagement at the Queens Club had been the first time Gregory shared a stage with acts that did not meet his approval, such as a shake dancer. He explained to one of his audiences that the only reason he continued to perform was because he was giving his salary to people in Mississippi. He was fired the next night, and he was convinced of the reason: "I guess it just bugged them that all that money was going down there."[50]

Gregory grew as an entertainer and activist based on his experiences in Mississippi. He likely developed new comedy material during his visits down south, such as his joke about a confused white amusement park owner in Mississippi: "He couldn't figure out where to seat Negroes on the merry-go-round."[51] Mainstream America continued to respond favorably to Gregory's method of ridiculing segregation and Jim Crow in the cultural arena, and his offstage activism gained equal recognition. "Hats off to comic Dick Gregory," a Chicago columnist wrote. "He is one of the few big name stars who is giving something other than lip service in the fight for Negro rights."[52] Gregory's willingness to dedicate himself to civil rights activism as much as he dedicated himself to show business was indeed exceptional. Several other African American celebrities made guest appearances and contributed to fundraising efforts, but their leadership and involvement in direct action initiatives often paled in comparison to Gregory's. His contributions are usually presented as scattered because he appeared at many points of battle, such as Birmingham, Alabama, for the private funeral services for four young girls killed in a church bombing, and in the nation's capital for the March on Washington. These presentations fail to properly separate Gregory's activities from those of many other socially conscious African American entertainers of the early 1960s. Gregory, more than any other entertainer, took the struggle for African American freedom to the local level, both in the North and South.

On January 1, 1964, Gregory joined a group of SNCC members in demanding service at three "whites-only" restaurants in Atlanta. Each was owned by Dobbs Houses, Inc., located in Memphis, Tennessee. Managers in Atlanta had been instructed not to call for the arrest of individuals participating in the sit-ins; instead, they were advised to prevent the possibility of racial violence by closing the establishments.[53] Twelve eateries owned by Dobbs were shut down during the period of demonstrations.

Gregory's wife, Lillian, and John Lewis, SNCC Chairman, were among twenty-five demonstrators jailed before Dobbs ownership began advising its store managers to refrain from calling law enforcement. They had spent Christmas behind bars but were released on January 2, 1964, when a "satisfactory agreement" between Dobbs and SNCC was announced.[54] J. K. Dobbs Jr., president of the company, delivered a statement indicating how difficult it would be to for African Americans to gain full equality in all of its 422 establishments:

> We have integrated in Atlanta and in some towns in Tennessee and Texas, but the company has no plans to integrate all its premises. A separate decision will be made in each place and the racial climate of the various parts of the country have much to do with each decision.[55]

The demonstrators in Atlanta achieved their goal by using a strategy popularized by college students in Greensboro, North Carolina. In 1960, four youth who attended North Carolina A&T University began "sitting in" at the lunch counter in the local Woolworth's department store. Although they were refused service based on the color of their skin, they returned day after day and remained until the store closed. Others, including whites, joined the sit-in. After nearly five months, Woolworth's agreed to serve African American customers at its lunch counters. "Sit-ins had occurred before, but never had they sparked so massive a response," historian Eric Foner argued. "The Greensboro sit-in launched the 1960s."[56] One of Gregory's jokes discussed his brother's and his own participation in the demonstrations designed to secure equal rights:

> My brother sat in a restaurant six months. He was so sure he wasn't going to get waited on he didn't bring any money with him. If they did serve him then they'd really have a reason to put him in jail.
> I was sitting in a restaurant 11 months once waiting for it to integrate. When they finally did integrate, they didn't have what I wanted.[57]

A month after helping to integrate Dobbs restaurant establishments in Atlanta, Gregory was arrested in Arkansas for "creating a disturbance at a truck-stop lunch counter by refusing to leave when asked by the management."[58] He was found guilty a week later, although confinement and fines failed to deter his activism. The only force capable of altering Gregory's steps was *himself*. He had not traveled to Arkansas to engage in direct action. His purpose had been to speak at a meeting of SNCC activists in Pine Bluff, but he insisted on stopping and entering Ray's Barbecue, "an all-night whites-only truck stop on the outskirts of town," before the meeting took place. William Hansen, one of his small group of hosts also jailed for refusing to leave the restaurant, characterized the pointless detour as "where the semi-insanity of working with Dick Gregory began."[59] It would not be the last time that one of Gregory's fiercely impulsive battle charges drew criticism from fellow activists.

In March 1964, Gregory warned officials in Princess Anne, Maryland—the first location where police dogs were unleashed on demonstrators—that he would call for "40 straight days of demonstrations" if the civil rights demands of its African American student population were not met.[60] Gregory's membership in ACT!, a new civil rights organization composed of the "most militant leaders in the Negro Revolution," provided more evidence of his aggressive approach to the race problem. About sixty like-minded activists, including Malcolm X and Gloria Richardson, met in Chester, Pennsylvania, to formalize the organization. Its sole qualification for membership was agreement with "direct action to resolve civil rights disputes."[61] Gregory was the only founding member with celebrity status. Although he was aware that affiliation with such a radical organization might jeopardize his unprecedented success in mainstream America, he pressed on. Fighting against segregation and Jim Crow had become his primary occupation.

On Friday, August 13, 1965, Gregory was shot. He suffered a bullet wound in his left thigh while attempting to mediate between law enforcement and a rioting crowd of African Americans in the Watts section of Los Angeles, California. Violence had erupted two nights before following the arrest of an African American motorist by a white officer for driving under the influence of alcohol. The incident was interpreted by many African Americans as continued harassment by police, and it ignited eight hours of protests. Tensions between law enforcement personnel and the thousands of African Americans in the streets grew too heavy to be contained. An Associated Press report described the chaotic scene:

> Scores of police cars, fire engines, ambulances and private autos were bombarded by bricks, stones and concrete. Officers chasing

rioters were mobbed and had to club their way to safety. At least a score of vehicles were overturned, several were burned and countless windshields shattered.[62]

On Friday morning before dawn, another dangerous confrontation between police and hundreds of African Americans took place. Many in the crowd were armed, and shots had been fired. Gregory risked his own life by stepping out to address the crowd because he feared a massacre was set to unfold. "I knew if I didn't go out in front," he explained, "the cops would start firing into the crowd of women and children."[63] It was then that he was struck by crossfire. Don Smith, chairman of the Congress of Racial Equality (CORE), was with Gregory, who had been told by police to take cover. Smith credited Gregory for his heroics: "It was the greatest display of courage I've ever seen. This stopped the shooting."[64]

Gregory was not the only activist injured by gunfire in 1965. Malcolm X was fatally wounded on February 21. Ossie Davis, an African American actor, gave a powerful, moving speech at his funeral. Among the thoughts Davis expressed was, "Malcolm was our manhood, our living, black manhood!"[65] The statement characterized most African Americans' perception of the aggressive approach Malcolm X adopted in the struggle for freedom. His forceful language, philosophy, and calls to action epitomized masculinity. Gregory was among those who linked verbal aggressiveness and direct action with manhood, and his satirical, biting humor reflected his politics of representation. He challenged racial inequality with his jokes, just as he challenged it with his participation.

The publication of his autobiography, *Nigger*, provided Gregory broader access to the American mainstream, and it personalized him as a man with a "moving story" who wanted "a world without hate and malice and is doing something about it."[66] The title was demonstrative of the shock effect in Gregory's act, and the dedication page showcased his humor that made it OK: "Dear Momma—Wherever you are, if ever you hear the word 'Nigger' again, remember they are advertising my book."[67] He had become both a leading entertainer and activist. Joseph Watkins Jr., a columnist for the *Defender*, asserted that Gregory had "no doubt taken over as the sole leader of the Negro people." Watkins shared his admiration for Gregory in no uncertain terms: "How often is it that a Negro, having made it, so to speak, turned his black back on his own black kind? Well, Dick has made it, has he weakened any? This man is wonderful."[68] Gregory's ascension as a race leader cost him opportunities, however. Dave Hepburn reported information "from more than one area" about Hollywood executives who had been seeking to cast African Americans in leading roles: "Talk was they were thinking of Dick Gregory, then discarded him on the basis of being too controversial."[69]

Cosby avoided the backlash that came with high visibility as a "race man." He seemingly sidestepped America's race problem on and off the comic stage. His debut comedy album, *Bill Cosby Is a Very Funny Fellow, Right!*, demonstrated his ability to take white listeners into urban Philadelphia without forcing them to consider the differences between themselves and their funnyman guide. Cosby's bit called "A Nut in Every Car" details the experience of riding Philadelphia's public rail system:

> I saw a three-act show from West 4th Street up to 125th Street. First act was this woman that went around condemning everyone. She got off at 23rd Street, she was so great we gave her a standing ovation. She got back on, did an encore up to 34th Street. At 34th Street she was replaced by 200 high school kids who went through the car, cut up the seats and the people.
>
> While I was enjoying this, I figured I'd go and look in the next car and see if they had a show going, and they did. They had a group participation show going, where everybody in the car was trying to pull in this one guy who had his leg caught in the doorway.
>
> So, I just dollied back into my [original] car and I saw that a crowd, just a crowd had grouped around, and I saw all these arms flailing and all this noise [sounds of karate chops]. And what I thought was a karate demonstration turned out to be two old ladies taking a seat from a wino.[70]

Cosby's strategic decision to forge a path as an African American comedian devoid of racial humor paid immediate dividends. First, it generated press, which worked to advance his career. He had established his own paradigm by becoming the "anti-Dick Gregory" of African American comedy, and columnists deemed the move newsworthy. "He is trying to make it as a funny man and as one whose color doesn't matter," the *Defender* noted.[71] A story in *Newsweek* suggested it was "startling" that Cosby's act included no material that could be classified as "strictly Negro jokes."[72] Cosby had invested considerable thought in developing his colorblind persona. He had become convinced that telling racial jokes to integrated audiences created division instead of unity between whites and African Americans. "Rather than trying to bring the races together by talking about differences," Cosby reasoned, "why not bring them together by talking about all the similarities?" The comedy shtick he spent several months perfecting was crafted to match his new aim: "I want to reach all the people."[73]

The second major benefit of Cosby's everyman approach to comedy was television marketability. Cosby's numerous appearances on programs hosted by the nation's leading talk-show personalities, such as Jack Paar, Johnny Carson, and Garry Moore, provide evidence of his widespread appeal to the networks' millions of viewers. Those in mainstream America who had not chosen to listen to race jokes on a record or at a live performance may have responded less favorably to Gregory's repeated bookings. But Cosby's neutral material, combined with Gregory's full-time work as an activist, likely explains why the former enjoyed greater television exposure by the end of 1963. He offered "Humor for Everyman."[74]

The long Civil Rights Movement also contributed to Cosby's rising stardom. African Americans had won tangible gains in the film and television industries, and white audiences had begun to welcome representations of African Americans that were not intended to reinforce a "white over black" social order. Sidney Poitier, America's first dark-skinned (and Bahamian-born) leading man on the big screen, enjoyed the freedom to "accept projects that furthered his objectives and presented positive images of blacks."[75] From his role as an African American doctor in *No Way Out* (1950) to his Oscar-winning portrayal of a do-good handyman in *Lilies of the Field* (1963), among countless others, Poitier's politics of representation worked well in aiding his ascendancy to the top of Hollywood. Like Cosby, he chose not to portray militancy with respect to civil rights. But his continued espousal of the clean-cut, nonthreatening African American male was not without consequence. Many African Americans, including fellow acting star Harry Belafonte, thought that Poitier's celebrity status could have been used to make stronger indictments against white supremacy. They assessed Poitier's refined public persona as a hindrance to the movement rather than a spark, and suggested that his pacified and desexualized image on the big screen represented emasculation, which ran counter to the larger aims of the struggle for African American freedom.

Cosby recalled similar criticisms. A feature article in *Ebony* suggested that his first television role presented him as a "'jovial, good-natured celibate' who can only be linked with one female—his mother," although the assessment was not offered with malicious intent.[76] With Gregory so deeply involved in civil rights causes, many in the media and general public expected Cosby, the only other African American comedian enjoying equal appeal among whites, to follow Gregory's fiery leadership. Ronald Smith relayed Cosby's reflections on the persistent questions regarding his lack of racial material and civil rights activism:

> I'm tired of those old jokes about stereotyped Negroes. You know what I mean? I don't miss Amos 'n' Andy. Second, I'm tired of those people who say, "You should be doing more to help your people." I'm a comedian, that's all. Third, my humor comes from the way I look at things. I am a man. I see things the way other people do. . . . A white person listens to my act and he laughs and he thinks, "Yeah, that's the way I see it, too." Okay. He's white. I'm Negro. And we both see things the same way. That must mean that *we are alike. Right?* So I figure this way I'm doing as much for good race relations as the next guy.[77]

Cosby's comments clearly outline his politics of representation, which ran counter to Gregory's. For Cosby, manhood lay not in challenging or ridiculing a prejudiced white person's views, but in modeling an African American man with familiar aspirations and concerns. He attempted to connect with white audience members using humor that highlighted his humanity rather than his race. This approach ushered in the second wave of a new cultural politics in the comic arena. While Gregory had mastered the domain of attacking segregation and Jim Crow directly, Cosby's method centered on likeability. He succeeded in constructing himself as not Dick Gregory, not a "race man," and not an agitator. The dichotomy between the comedians belongs in historical debates on twentieth-century strategies for African American uplift.

Other African Americans joined Cosby in benefiting from the civil rights gains of the 1960s and taking advantage of the opportunity to market their talents. "You don't notice the difference on television this season?" Jesse H. Walker asked in his popular entertainment column. "Pick any given night at random and mark how many Negroes you will notice." Walker's objective was to highlight the increased visibility of African American entertainers, such as Sammy Davis Jr., Ethel Waters, Ossie Davis, Cicely Tyson, and Bill Cosby, on network television. "That's progress," he concluded.[78] He noted that the next step was for African American entertainers to become regulars on television programs rather than occasional guests. Cosby's delightful humor as Johnny Carson's guest on *The Tonight Show* demonstrated why he would soon become the first African American to receive such an opportunity:

> I actually feel sorry for the Wolf Man. Here's a guy who can't remember when the moon's gonna come up on him. And he must be awfully embarrassing to his family. You know, he's sitting around the table eating, and up comes the moon.
>
> [Family Members:] *Aww. Go on out in the yard some place, and get out of here!*
>
> And it must be embarrassing to watch him in a barber shop getting a haircut straight, you know, and all of a sudden, up comes the wolf.
>
> [Barber:] *That's gonna cost you an extra eight dollars there.*
>
> [Wolf Man:] Well, make it light around the legs, will ya please?[79]

Cosby's popularity, opportunities, and earnings increased following his breakout year. In January 1964, he served as guest host of *The Tonight Show* while Carson was on vacation. In November, his sophomore comedy album, *I Started Out as a Child*, went on sale and sold 150,000 copies within a year.[80] Cosby continued avoiding the issue of race on the record, which was taped at Mister Kelly's nightclub in Chicago. Reviews that included excerpts of his humor failed to convey the pleasure of experiencing his act in person, as physical gestures and voice effects were major components of his performances. Cosby's bit about the diet of Neanderthals was one of several that invited the live audience into the vacuum of his imagination:

> I figure, the only thing that they know how to eat—the bushes were there for them, so they just ate bushes, everyday, bushes. And they must have gotten tired of bushes.
>
> [Neanderthal:] *Aww, this is rotten. These bushes, they're the worst bush I've ever had in my life. Don't eat that bush because it'll make you get a rash. You'll break right out. It's terrible.*

And the guy would go home from a hard day's work, and he'd say, *What's for dinner?*

[Wife:] Bushes.

[Neanderthal:] *Aww, bushes! I'll die first. I'd rather die first than eat bushes!*

So then he had to go out and get something else. So some guy says, *Hey, why don't we try meat?* And the guy says, *OK.* So that's when they went out. Now they must have made a couple of mistakes, see. They must have attacked the wrong animals. So we see, basking away in the sun, two saber tooth tigers. And one of the tigers talks to the other.

[Tiger #1:] Hey, Arnold.

[Tiger #2:] *Yeah?*

[Tiger #1:] Don't look now, but over your right shoulder there's a Neanderthal man sneaking up on us, and he's got a stick in his hand, and he's gonna hit one of us.

[Tiger #2:] *Say what?*

[Tiger #1:] That's the same nut that hit me behind the ear with a rock and run like hell yesterday. You know they killed Ralphie yesterday.

[Tiger #2:] *Ralphie? Who's Ralphie?*

[Tiger #1:] You know Ralphie, that weird saber tooth tiger, that was over the hill. He only had his one saber, and he growls with a lisp. He says, *Aaarspth!* They killed him yesterday.

[Tiger #2:] *Oh, that's terrible!*

[Tiger #1:] Yep. Then they cut his fur off and they threw him in the fire.

[Tiger #2:] *Oh, that's horrible!*

[Tiger #1:] Yeah, and they drug him out of the fire, and they ate him!

[Tiger #2:] *What a bunch of savages!*

[Tiger #1:] I tell you what we'll do. Let's get up and start growling and making a whole bunch of noise, alright? (Sounds of tigers roaring) What's he doing now?

[Tiger #2:] *He's eating bushes, that's what he's doing.*[81]

Cosby had worked hard to build mass appeal that crossed racial boundaries, and his efforts proved successful. His habit of being less than forthcoming with the media began during this period. He viewed the idea of expressing candid thoughts against white supremacy as detrimental to his career and counter to his personal politics. Cosby had established the image of a happy child turned playful adult who harbored no animosity based on America's race problem. Reporters uncovered no controversial information about the comedian beyond this public persona. "Cos would deflect questions about his childhood and marriage as much as possible," Ronald Smith noted. "He wanted to let the warm, funny stories of growing up be accepted as fictionalized fact."[82] Interviewers became aware of his tendency to dodge personal questions. "A conversation with Cosby is an engagingly cluttered affair," Helen Dudar shared with her readers. "Verbally, he rarely goes anyplace in a straight line if he can detour."[83] Lillian Calhoun observed the same in her interview of the twenty-six-year-old comedian and his new bride, Camille Hanks. Cosby had set the tone by lying across the bed of his hotel suite. "Interviews with comedians should be funny," she wrote, "but this one was ridiculous."[84]

Calhoun managed to extract greater insight from Cosby regarding his politics of representation on stage. The comedian reiterated his method of achieving racial harmony by focusing on similarities between African Americans and whites rather than differences:

> There is no great difference between an American Negro and white Americans. When I do my piece on street football: "I have one guy run behind the black Chevy to catch the ball. I send another one in my living room to receive a pass. I tell another to run take the bus and have the driver leave the door

open so I can fake a pass . . ." Many of the white men out there laughing in the audience have had the same experience.

Cosby had explained his tactic of employing nonaggressive, nonracial humor as an aid in the struggle for African American freedom. He had not avoided the subject of race to completely remove himself from the landscape of civil rights activism. He had, in fact, joined it on his own terms. Cosby complemented his complex form of activism onstage with behind-the-scenes support of resistance efforts offstage. He contributed financially to the fight to dismantle segregation and Jim Crow, and he encouraged others to do the same, "even if it's only a quarter."[85] He also donated his talent to fundraisers hosted by social and political organizations. In May 1964, Cosby joined Dick Gregory, Lena Horne, Ossie Davis, Eartha Kitt, Harry Belafonte, and dozens more African American entertainers for a televised NAACP "Freedom Spectacular," which sought to raise one million dollars to advance civil rights causes.[86] While he repeatedly projected the self-image of a colorless comedian and individual, Cosby was very much an African American man aware of and pushing against the race problem in America.

The culmination of Cosby's grand scheme occurred in 1965 when he was cast as the first African American to star in a dramatic television series, *I Spy*. Sheldon Leonard, the white executive producer of the program, handpicked Cosby to portray one of two highly educated, multilingual spies after watching the comedian perform on a television variety show. "The part was conceived for a white man—but a whole man, a man of humor, physical fitness and competence," Leonard said. But Cosby's talent and charm led to an epiphany, and Sheldon soon contacted a network executive to discuss his intent to offer the role to "a young comedian who had every quality we were looking for."[87] Journalist Stanley Karnow asserted that Cosby's role was not one initially intended to launch a "racial revolution" in television. "At the outset," Karnow concluded based on interviews with entertainment insiders, "Cosby was slated to play the familiar Negro role of second banana to the white star, Bob Culp. But as the drive for civil rights gathered momentum, the image of a Negro as a full-fledged costar began to look better, and Cosby's part in *I Spy* was gradually upgraded."[88]

Regardless of the original intent of Cosby's inclusion in *I Spy*, the comedian was informed of Leonard's final vision for his role and its place in America's social milieu. Cosby credited Leonard for thinking "it was time that a Negro and a white could play together in a series that did not have any racial overtones."[89] This preference likely ruled out consideration of Gregory. His politics of representation onstage and highly publicized civil rights activism offstage made his image synonymous with race and social activism.

The New York Society for Ethical Culture (NYSEC), a social justice organization, issued a report in 1962 criticizing the television industry for its failure to include African Americans in daily programs. The report credited the industry for airing documentaries that highlighted civil rights issues and increasing the representation of African Americans in commercials, but it condemned the "lily-white" regular television programming that largely excluded African American actors. Douglas Pugh, co-chair of the society's Committee on Integration, explained the report's findings: "About 100 of our members monitored television for two weeks. Their survey showed that Negro appearances were insufficient for our times, and this was in New York—a liberal state."[90] Jesse Walker agreed with the critical summary provided by NYSEC. "The distortion of the American scene is so unfair on daytime TV," he charged, "that if you watch it constantly you'd wonder if Negroes lived in these United States." He suggested that Cosby's casting on *I Spy* was a positive step, but that it was primarily a "defensive mechanism" by the network in response to the NYSEC report.[91] The undertaking of the report, its findings, and its reception indicate the controversy surrounding the representation of African Americans on network television in the mid-1960s.

In *Prime Time Blues: African Americans on Network Television*, Donald Bogle argues that concerns about reactions from sponsors and white viewers delayed the regular television appearance of "average" African American individuals and families until the 1970s. While guest appearances by African Americans on special programs that featured attitudes about the struggle for freedom were common before this point, Bogle's investigation reveals that the path African Americans traveled to inclusion in the television industry was a highly contested one that did not end with Cosby's portrayal of international spy Alexander Scott. Bogle demonstrates the importance of "the tube" in the lives of millions of American families, as his research shows that "while only 3 percent of American households had television sets in 1949, 24 percent of homes had the tube by 1954. By 1956, the number had grown to 72 percent."[92] The rapid growth of the new medium carried the potential to correct many white Americans' assumptions about African Americans based on stereotypical characters from earlier radio programs (and the enduring legacy of slavery). In this regard, Cosby's groundbreaking role shattered the familiar portrayal of African Americans as shiftless buffoons and replaced it with the image of a man characterized by intelligence, versatility, and professionalism.

Robert Culp, a veteran white actor, had previously accepted the starring role on *I Spy* opposite Cosby. Together the two men would portray CIA agents traveling the world under the cover of a tennis player (Culp) and his trainer/companion (Cosby). Television industry insiders had long speculated that the first African American to star in a series would need to do so opposite a white star. "This, they think, the sponsors will buy. Not the other," Dave Hepburn noted.[93] Many may have been surprised in the fall of 1965 when Cosby transformed into Alexander Scott, a character he recalled enjoying because Scott "wears a tie, has brains and shows the Negro being himself, a human being."[94] There was no stereotyping or "Uncle Tom-ing" associated with the role. Cosby's politics of representation would have led him to decline the role had he found it racially specific, just as he had previously declined television appearances that asked him to discuss racial issues. Culp addressed the difficulty of those in the media who "couldn't find the relationship" between him and Cosby on screen: "They all tried to put me in the front seat and Cosby in the back seat and that wasn't the idea. We are actually almost mirror images of each other. Sometimes I take the back seat and sometimes Bill does."[95] Cosby's projected neutrality on the race issue had certainly assisted him in landing the part, and the role itself contributed to advancing the American public toward envisioning a society in which African American and white men could coexist with equality and harmony. Considered too early by some and too late by others, the program may have aired at just the right time.

It is difficult to assess the degree to which Cosby considered his casting on *I Spy* as a victory in the struggle for African American freedom. He won three successive Emmy Awards for best actor and advanced America's readiness for interracial casting on prime-time television, but he faced criticism for portraying a character that many viewed as a "black man playing a white man." The more militant ranks of African Americans demanded that Cosby demonstrate race pride and highlight racial oppression through his art. "How long would a series last if it really told it like it is?" Cosby asked in response to the idea. "The industry itself knows what it wants to do: it wants to make money. The industry is not interested in the true story of Benjamin Banneker or Malcolm X."[96] Cosby learned this lesson very early in his career, and it became his primary consideration as he balanced the relationship between entertainment and civil rights.

"I entered show business to make money, not to lead a march," Cosby said during the first season of *I Spy*.[97] "Money is of the utmost importance to me," he explained in a separate interview.[98] Cosby further distanced himself from the expectation of overt activism by contrasting his qualifications with those of his immediate predecessor: "Gregory's motives are genuine. He believes in freedom, he believes in the movement, he'll go anywhere to do a benefit. I'm not bright enough to lead." Cosby rationalized his absences from protests that carried the potential for violence: "I just can't see praying for someone who's kicking you and I don't want to go where there's tear gas unless I have some tear gas to throw back at them."[99]

By no means did Cosby possess the same strain of activism as Gregory. Their motivations were different, as the former privileged financial success to a far greater degree than the latter. However, Cosby was indeed cognizant of his social significance and alternative contributions to the struggle that Gregory and thousands of other activists waged on the front lines. And one comment Cosby made in October 1965 is as profound as it is contradictory, considering his publicly professed aim in show business. After discussing the experience of traveling overseas to film episodes of *I Spy* and feeling "respected and protected" as an African American entertainer, he momentarily dropped the reference to money as a motivating factor: "I'm financially a big success, I guess. But I realize that the money doesn't really matter. It's the dignity I'm working for."[100]

I Spy was filmed on location around the world. With a budget of $4.5 million, it was "one of the most expensive TV series ever produced."[101] The program aired on 182 stations across America, which was 96 percent of the NBC network. The local station in New York received 174 calls regarding the show during its first season; 122 were approving.[102] Perhaps no accolade was more resounding than that offered by James Hicks, who considered Cosby a "Negro Hero":

> I tell you, it's truly wonderful!
>
> Can you imagine what this means to Negroes? All these years we've been sitting on the edges of our seats watching a handful of "good" Negroes on television, wishing they would do something spectacular.

But the "good" Negroes always went through their little shining hours and then took a kick in the tail from some bad white man and off they went into a corner to die like all "good" Negroes die on television.

But now all of a sudden, we have a good "bad" Negro hero on television with a gun in his hand who doesn't die and who can do no wrong.

Instead of slinking off to die in a corner as the curtain fades, Bill Cosby stands there waving his trusty gun while the announcer tells you what he is going to shoot up next week. I tell you, it's truly wonderful![103]

For many, Cosby's success in television produced feelings of racial pride like those that followed Joe Louis's defeat of Max Schmeling. He had achieved such a meteoric rise in just three years. The liner notes to his third album, *Why Is There Air?*, suggested a reason for his swift climb: "Bill Cosby has fingers like tentacles, talks faster than a scared mule, and has a heart bigger than Dumbo, the Flying Pink Elephant. Mules and tentacles are fine. But that heart, man, is the gas. That's one of the qualities that makes Bill so Cosby. Makes him so warmly accepted."[104] He had become the "Jackie Robinson of TV" in no small part because of a politics of representation that projected neutrality with respect to race and civil rights and commonality with respect to childhood and family life.[105] It worked in separating him from Gregory, the nation's first African American professional stand-up comedian to experience mainstream success, and it dissociated him from a new strain of the Civil Rights Movement—Black Power. This philosophy carried with it the worst-case scenario of major bloodshed in the name of freedom. Both Gregory and Cosby faced the question of whether Black Power ideology was the best path toward African American freedom. Their methods in supporting its aims, much like their politics of representation, were stark opposites.

Dick Gregory takes a break at SIU band practice, November 26, 1956 (Rip Stokes Photograph Collection, Morris Library, Special Collections Research Center, Southern Illinois University Carbondale)

Bill Cosby holding a javelin at Temple track and field practice, ca. 1960s (John W. Mosley Photograph Collection, Charles L. Blockson Afro-American Collection, Temple University Libraries, Philadelphia, PA)

Dick Gregory being interviewed on *The Mike Douglas Show*, 1965 (Everett Collection)

Bill Cosby performing a stand-up routine during *The Second Bill Cosby Special*, April 9, 1969 (Everett Collection)

Ossie Davis (left) and Dick Gregory, members of the National Coalition against War, Racism and Repression, speak to reporters at United Nations Plaza, New York City, November 16, 1970 (Everett Collection)

Sidney Poitier (left) and Bill Cosby in *Let's Do It Again*, 1975 (Everett Collection)

Chapter 4

Black Comedy, Black Power

On April 4, 1968, Dick Gregory learned of Martin Luther King Jr.'s assassination just before delivering a lecture in California. He remembered the faces of the Hartnell College students he spoke to that evening as being "in shock." Gregory, who increasingly focused on touring the nation's college campuses, was not; "I'm sure if you asked anyone who marched with him they would tell you that they were not shocked by Dr. King's assassination. After they blew up the Sixteenth Street Baptist Church in Birmingham in September 1963, we were prepared for the worst."[1] King's death further radicalized Gregory. He began to gather evidence to prove that government officials had plotted to kill not only King, but John F. Kennedy and himself.[2]

By 1968, Gregory had voluntarily moved away from a career path that would have led to greater opportunities and income. He upset white club owners by requiring them to employ African American waiters during his engagements.[3] He vehemently protested America's involvement in Vietnam and, upon paying his own travel costs to the war zone, refused to entertain troops who fought on the front lines because he deemed it equivalent to "entertaining a convention to bank robbers."[4] He fished by net with Native Americans in the state of Washington in protest of government regulation of their "traditional fishing rights," and he dropped to 110 pounds while executing a hunger strike during his jail sentence.[5] Appearing on a Chicago radio program in 1967, he predicted that the United States would be burned down by 1970. The Mississippi Sovereignty Commission called it a "vicious threat" from a "lunatic," a man "linked with Stokely Carmichael who is dedicated to the destruction of America."[6]

There was very little surprise when Gregory defended the latter's calls for Black Power:

> The most obscene words black people have used for the past two hundred years are "m.f." Negroes are always "m.f.n'" something—m.f. tree or m.f. job. But a white newspaper never ran an editorial about the use of those two words. You never heard the New York Times say, *"Why don't Negroes stop using those two words. Mother is a very sacred word in American society."* Yet when we get two clean words together like "black" and "power," which even the Pope can use, newspapers try to say they are the most obscene words we ever came across.[7]

Bill Cosby, too, identified with aspects of Black Power, but he channeled them toward his professional success. The emerging comedy legend subscribed to a politics of representation that avoided antagonizing whites with his race consciousness, although he strategically worked the fight for African American equality into his blossoming entertainment career. Cosby championed the "Black Is Beautiful" component of Black Power ideology when he told the *London Times* that he would "never hold or kiss a white woman" onscreen because he wanted to be seen "only with our women—not Chinese or Filipino women, not yellow, green, pink, or white. Just our women, black ones."[8] But his statement also worked to reaffirm his status as a "safe" African American celebrity, one who had no interest in dismantling racial taboos. The daring statement carried little sting among mainstream America because of the pleasantly and amazingly broad appeal that distinguished him among African American comedians:

> I guess most of you know I have two daughters, my family, which I did not ask for. I asked my wife for sons. I looked at her, yes I did. I said *"you will give me sons. Repeat after me: you will."* And I have daughters now. My wife tried to blame it on me. "Well, you know the male carries the determining factor. He carries the Y and the X chromosomes." Yeah? Bull. 'Cause in my philosophy, it's the person's fault who last had it![9]

Cosby knew that his style was a winner, especially in contrast to Gregory's. "Dick has always been a specifically Negro comedian in the sense that his material comes from the fact that he's Negro," he charged.

"Mine doesn't."[10] Cosby used his entertainment capital to make unprecedented strides in television, film, and society. In less than a two-month period, his comedy albums sold more than one million copies. *New York Daily News* reported that Cosby was "so thrilled with his record news that he purchased a Cadillac convertible for his manager, Roy Silver."[11] Unbeknownst to most, Cosby executed an impressive plan for African American uplift that he kept out of the headlines by design and necessity. His "cultural passing" worked masterfully. On the evening of King's assassination, Cosby told a packed Kansas audience that he just could not continue the comedy concert that they had paid to see. They stood and applauded "until it seemed they couldn't applaud enough."[12]

By 1966, the long Civil Rights Movement had reached a turning point as angry black bodies decorated the American landscape and peppered its political climate. While most African Americans recognized the progress made in the post–World War II period—establishment of the Fair Employment Practices Commission, rendering of the *Brown* verdict, passage of the Civil Rights and Voting Rights Acts—many remained dissatisfied and demanded more rapid strides toward equality. Ideological conflicts between movement and organizational leaders clearly indicate that the struggle for African American freedom experienced an internal struggle for direction. Stokely Carmichael emerged as the forceful, charismatic drum major who would communicate its message to the black masses and American mainstream. Following his arrest for trespassing on the civil rights trail in Greenwood, Mississippi, his rhetoric reflected the attitudes of growing numbers of African Americans ready to consider more aggressive strategies, including the use of violent resistance to combat violent oppression: "This is the 27th time I have been arrested. I ain't going to jail no more, I ain't going to jail no more." Carmichael further proclaimed the new aim of America's angriest citizens when he repeatedly chanted, "We want black power!"[13]

The event that landed Carmichael in Mississippi was the March Against Fear, which began on June 5, 1966, as a solo effort by James Meredith, the University of Mississippi's first African American matriculate. Meredith planned to march roughly 220 miles from the Peabody Hotel in Memphis, Tennessee, to Jackson, Mississippi, in protest against the largely unchecked physical and psychological terror that southern white supremacists wielded against African Americans. Increasing the number of African American registered voters in Mississippi factored heavily into Meredith's campaign. Yet just one day into the march, Meredith was shot.

As quickly as he was hospitalized, his ill-advised strike against racial inequality transformed into an organized, multitiered battle. Leaders of the freedom struggle, including Carmichael, King, and Floyd McKissick, national director of CORE, descended upon Mississippi to complete the march to Jackson. Gregory contributed his star power and leadership to the effort, which was renamed the Meredith March, and led a small contingency from the Mississippi highway spot at which Meredith was wounded back to Memphis.

Gregory's familiarity with the racial politics of the South, particularly Mississippi, stemmed from years of agitation. "It seemed no matter where the Movement took me," he wrote, "I always ended up back in Mississippi, where it had all begun for me."[14] Since accepting an invitation from Medgar Evers to appear at a 1962 NAACP protest rally in Jackson, Gregory internalized African American Mississippians' local struggle for freedom. It was at this rally that he took in the words of an elderly man fresh out of jail who preceded him at the podium: "I don't mind going to jail for freedom, no, I wouldn't even mind being killed for freedom. But my wife and I was married a long time, and, well, you know I ain't never spent a night away from home. While I was in jail, my wife died."[15] Gregory credited the story with igniting his work as a civil rights crusader despite the very real threat such activism posed to his livelihood and *life*.

The Meredith March again demonstrated Gregory's willingness to serve on the movement's dangerous front lines. Mississippi patrolmen had failed to prevent the attack on Meredith, which certainly punctuated the level of risk. King asserted that Meredith's shooting was "indicative of the fact that a reign of terror still exists in the South."[16] White supremacists attempted to intimidate Meredith with insults and spitting, and even the sight of his white attacker carrying a shotgun struck law enforcement on the scene as "not unusual." Friends of Meredith advised him against marching through Mississippi. Lee Meredith, the white sheriff of Desoto County, located just below the Tennessee state line, predicted that "the trouble will come when he reaches Panola County. That's where our big Klux activity is."[17] Sheriff Meredith either underestimated or attempted to downplay the racism present in his jurisdiction, as James Meredith's shooter, who later pled guilty to assault and battery with intent to kill, wounded the activist in the heart of DeSoto County.[18] Despite these logical deterrents, Gregory's feet were on the ground at the spot where James Meredith had been injured fewer than twenty-four hours later. Joined by his wife, Lillian, and five friends, Gregory was "the first to restart the freedom walk."[19]

By 1966, Gregory had fathered five children: Michele, Lynn, Pamela and Paula (twins), and Stephanie. His consideration of the United States they would inherit drove his participation in the struggle for African American freedom, and he never lost sight of the better society that he believed his generation owed to those who would follow. Gregory admonished those African Americans who did not similarly internalize the fight for equality. In his autobiography, he reflected on a verbal exchange that took place shortly after one of the most disturbing acts of racial violence during the 1960s—a church bombing in Birmingham, Alabama, that left four African American adolescent girls dead:

> I talked to the father of one of the kids who died in that church in Birmingham. He said to me: "You know, Gregory, my daughter begged me to let her demonstrate, and I told her no. I told her she was too young. And she looked at me, and she said: 'Then you do it, Daddy.'"
>
> And that's what that man will have to live with for the rest of his life. Because if Birmingham [youth] had had enough [adult] Negroes behind them, there wouldn't have been a bombing.[20]

Gregory's immediate response to the shooting of James Meredith reinforced his ideas about the role of all African Americans, including those in the celebrity and middle-class ranks, in the movement. It also brought to life one of his comedy bits about having urged his mother to become more politically active when he was a child. After Mrs. Gregory purportedly told young Dick that she cared more about *his* eventual enjoyment of equal rights rather than her own, he responded, "Mama, get 'em for *yourself* and I know I got 'em!"[21]

On Tuesday, June 7, 1966, Gregory's leadership of one segment of the Meredith March continued his strides toward a more equitable society. Apart from the coalition of activists that carried on Meredith's 220-mile southward journey to Jackson, Gregory's band traveled in the opposite direction. Forty African American residents of DeSoto County flanked his twenty-six mile northward march from Hernando, Mississippi, to Memphis. Gregory's decision not to join Carmichael, King, and McKissick on the longer route to Jackson may have been due to his close personal relationship with Meredith, who held serious reservations about others co-opting *his* march. Aram Goudsouzian's detailed study of the march recounts Meredith's reluctance to endorse the plans of those big names who rushed to Mississippi to wave the banner of freedom: "Would a big march make life difficult for poor black Mississippians? Would women and children face danger? Would discipline and order be maintained over two hundred miles, four times the distance from Selma to Montgomery?"[22] Gregory was Meredith's first celebrity visitor, and he was loyal to the wishes of his good friend to whom he felt the movement owed so much. "I felt indebted to him—we all were," Gregory remembered. "He had walked the treacherous halls of [the University of Mississippi] for the benefit of all our children."[23] Additionally, Gregory's obligation to serve a weeklong prison stint for charges related to his civil disobedience in Illinois a year prior likely factored into his decision not to spend the next couple of weeks participating in the marches to Jackson.[24]

Gregory's group reached Memphis after roughly eight hours of marching, and a wrap-up rally at Centenary Methodist Church featured speeches by movement leaders that "underscored their differences," or rather highlighted the growing chasm between traditional civil rights activists and an increasingly militant segment. Whitney Young, director of the National Urban League, acknowledged the movement's methodological divide yet posited that its leaders were "united as one on man's right to walk down the highways unmolested."[25] The ideological divide mirrored the widening divergence between Gregory and Cosby. Gregory sacrificed hundreds of thousands of dollars annually by the mid-1960s in travel, donations, canceled or lost bookings/roles, legal fees, and research/reporting (he maintained a team of up to twelve journalists to investigate civil rights abuses across the nation), while Cosby climbed the celebrity ladder by rejecting public identification as a race man. Although he made notable donations and appearances at special events, by no means would he be characterized by the public as an agitator.

Juxtaposing the humor and activism of Cosby and Gregory in the mid-1960s reveals ideologies as contrasting as King's and Carmichael's. While King's followers in the Meredith March shouted "Freedom," Carmichael's followers shouted "Uhuru," the Swahili word for "freedom."[26] Black Power encouraged political and cultural reidentification with Africa as part of its radical agenda for advancement. The use of an African language indicated resistance against white oppressors whose ancestors had forbade generations of Africans in North America from communicating using their native languages. "Freedom!" versus "Uhuru!" served as a surface-level representation of the deep split between the traditional nonviolent group and the new militant strain. Charles Evers, older brother of the slain Mississippi activist Medgar Evers, echoed the sentiments of many who embraced Black Power when he commented on Meredith's shooting: "There are many Negroes who now feel the only time we are going to get response and action is when we start shooting whites, and many of them are ready to do it. If I'd been James Meredith and that white man cut loose on me with a shotgun, I'd have been shooting back."[27] In Harlem, speakers who addressed a crowd in front of the Hotel Theresa in the wake of Meredith's shooting were constantly interrupted by a man who screamed that they should "get some guns and go down and retaliate."[28] Meredith, too, expressed thoughts in line with those who advocated a change from strict adherence to civil disobedience. Speaking to reporters two weeks after being shot, he said, "If the government refuses to protect Negroes, there is no choice left to the Negro but to provide protection for himself. A man should never be helpless."[29]

The belief in violent resistance to violent oppression characterized Black Power activists in the American mainstream more than any other feature. Isolated acts of violence by African Americans against whites who threatened their liberty and safety had occurred well before the 1960s, but the new mass ideology of meeting force with force raised fears of unfathomable bloodshed among both races. "We find proven once again that words will not stop bullets," Carmichael explained to Meredith's family via telegram following his shooting.[30] "Our grandfathers had to run, run, run," he reminded a West Coast audience in 1967. "My generation has run out of breath. We just ain't running no more!"[31]

Black Power carried far more in ideology than the belief in armed self-defense, such as community development, labor rights, universal health care, and prison reform. But the new mass promotion of armed resistance appealed to those who desired a more rapid pace of change. John Lewis, chairman of SNCC from 1963 until the controversial election of Carmichael in May 1966, rejected the militant surge: "It was doing more to destroy the movement and to destroy the coalition that I thought we had built."[32] Lewis's commitment to nonviolence precluded his participation in a program that espoused violence, even in self-defense. His eventual divorce from SNCC demonstrated his belief that Black Power divided African Americans in the movement and "widened the gulf between blacks and whites in this country."[33] It may have been too soon for Lewis to recognize that "pluralists" within the Black Power movement aimed to "share political control, not to dominate, humiliate, or exclude other competing groups."[34] Regardless, Lewis was not alone. King warned of the potentially disastrous consequences of Black Power. "Tragedy has many forms," he expressed on behalf of SCLC. "Among them could be the needless harm of a just cause by an extremism within the Civil Rights Movement that rivals the excesses of its opponents."[35] Gregory understood both sides: "I'm nonviolent, but I'll be damned if I'll preach non-violence to a man whose five-year-old daughter has got her head busted open by a brick."[36] His decision to endorse those in favor of violent resistance contributed to his perceived radicalism and decreasing favorability with mainstream America.

Meredith left the William B. Bowld hospital in Memphis three days after suffering gunshot wounds and returned to his home in New York.[37] He rejoined the march he started after traveling back to Mississippi a couple of weeks later on June 24. Notwithstanding the criticism he received for having displayed "appalling" naiveté and apparent ignorance of "white-Negro Mississippi relations which is etched in the Negroes' blood across the length and breadth of that unholy state," his campaign had resulted in an important gathering of the most influential leaders in the struggle for African American freedom.[38] Gregory, who had also been away from Mississippi for a couple of weeks, reconnected with Meredith in St. Louis and accompanied his friend back to the battleground state that served as the foundation of their comradery. The two participated in a short march from Canton, Mississippi, to the campus of Tougaloo College, a small campus in North Jackson that had served African American students for nearly a century.

Gregory emceed the star-studded gathering on June 25, which included Sammy Davis Jr., Marlon Brando, Frank Sinatra, and James Brown among its long list of entertainers.[39] James Coleman, a Tougaloo graduate who had returned to the college to serve as athletic director and dean of men, recalled highlights from the inspiring evening, such as James Brown flying in on a private jet and Sammy Davis Jr. arriving in a helicopter that landed on the college's football field. Dean Coleman assisted the effort by opening Tougaloo's facilities to the masses of supporters present, which he estimated to be "somewhere in the neighborhood of 30,000 or 40,000 people."[40] It was a grand spectacle that carried more meaning than any ordinary concert. Thousands had come to stand with African American Mississippians in demanding progress.

A Toledo, Ohio, newspaper ran a story on June 26 titled "Civil Rights Chiefs Close Ranks Behind Meredith." The article accurately recorded the discord among key activists in Mississippi, which heightened with Meredith's return. King and others had marched to the Tougaloo campus by the time Meredith made it to Canton, Mississippi, on Friday, June 24. Meredith felt snubbed—it was *his* march, after all—and led another group of 500 marchers from Canton to Tougaloo on Saturday, June 25. In an effort to show a united front, King led a group of 400 people already at Tougaloo's campus to meet Meredith's group so that they could march back to the college together. King explained that there had been a "temporary breakdown in communications."[41]

The communications breakdown may have grown more widespread had Gregory not intervened. On the campus of Tougaloo College, as each civil rights organization attempted to conduct private strategy sessions for upcoming marches, Gregory applied the weight that his participation in the movement commanded toward connecting leaders with conflicting agendas. According to Dean Coleman, "it was Dick Gregory who was really responsible for pulling all the groups together."[42] Gregory employed the tool of humor to bridge even trivial divides, such as the difference between northerners' and southerners' dialects. He told the thousands of Mississippians in the audience that "when y'all get to saying it real fast down here, it sounds like you're saying 'Black Powder!' Now, you don't want to mess around and make the Klu Kluck Klan think y'all calling them." When Sammy Davis Jr. took the stage to entertain the crowd, Gregory humorously apologized to his fellow celebrity for what may have been perceived as too small of an audience for Davis's star power. "I want to apologize to Sammy," he said, "because, Sammy, this is a heck of a crowd out there, and the only reason there's not more is because Mississippi State Police is outside stopping people from getting in. But they gon' get here!"[43]

On a midsummer weekend during which he had earned amounts between $10,000 and $50,000 in years prior, Gregory sacrificed the possibility of such earnings in favor of direct action against Jim Crow. Journalist Adolph Slaughter identified Gregory as continuing his record of "stellar contributions to the civil rights struggle."[44] Despite all of the star power that Meredith's march amassed, none of the millionaires who helped make its closing events a success matched Gregory's physical, emotional, or financial involvement in the fight against Jim Crow. Charles Evers recalled that "Dick Gregory was one of us."

Cosby stayed away from the march as weekly episodes of *I Spy* entertained those Americans living more "normal" lives in June 1966. In Evers's view, Cosby's absence did not minimize his contributions to the movement. Although Evers did not recall Cosby having ever visited Mississippi as part of any civil rights effort, he concluded that "it wasn't necessary for everybody to march. Bill's money helped get those of us who did out of jail."[45] Had he been present, Cosby may not have publicly aligned himself with the likes of Carmichael, the nation's new popular radical. The tone of Carmichael's and other leaders' explanation of Black Power definitions seemed incongruent with Cosby's politics of representation, even though he supported its larger aim:

> Black Power is not just a mere slogan, nationally or internationally. It is real that black people can come together and start determining for [themselves] how they're going to live, and controlling their economic and political lives.[46]
>
> —Stokely Carmichael

> It means dignity. It doesn't mean violence. It means integrity. It doesn't mean anti-whites. It means pride in being black. It means you're willing to cooperate with your white brother and sister, if they're going to cooperate with you, in terms of giving you the same things that they have.[47]
>
> —Adam Clayton Powell, Jr.

> Black Power is no mere slogan. It is a movement dedicated to the exercise of American democracy in its highest tradition; it is a drive to mobilize the Black communities of this country in a monumental effort to remove the basic causes of alienation, frustration, despair, low self-esteem and hopelessness.[48]
>
> —Floyd McKissick

> If anyone wants to know what black power means let him pick up a dictionary and look up the word "black" and the word "power"—then you get it, baby.[49]
>
> —Dick Gregory

In 1967, Gregory campaigned for the office of mayor of Chicago. Drew Pearson, a reporter for the *New York Post*, described the election as one of two "knockdown, drag-out political battles" in Illinois.[50] When asked to reveal the first thing he would do if elected, Gregory responded, "I'll post a $100,000 reward for my own arrest for any wrongdoing in office."[51] Like most Black Power activists, Gregory viewed the white power structure in Chicago under incumbent Mayor Richard Daley as part of a system that privileged whites and oppressed African Americans—an obvious injustice. Pearson determined that "the Chicago race will decide whether a Negro can take control from a firmly entrenched [white] Democratic boss of a big city machine."[52] Gregory failed, and his campaign stood as one of several "quixotic, symbolic, and, in the end, futile" mayoral bids by African American Chicagoans until former state senator Harold Washington broke through in 1983.[53] Yet Gregory put a positive spin on the roughly 22,000 write-in votes he won: "I am the Independent Write-In Mayor of Chicago in Exile."[54]

Gregory's debt began to mount, reaching a high of $200,000 due in no small part to "maintaining a crusading itinerary that keeps him buried."[55] One journalist posited in 1967 that "Dick Gregory, widely known as comedian Dick Gregory, hasn't got a funny bone in his head."[56] The comment reflected Gregory's move toward activism and away from entertainment. Ralph Mann, Gregory's manager, estimated that his civil rights involvement since 1962 had come at a cost of more than $1 million. Gregory did not care. "Capitalism respects only wealth, not human values," he charged. "I was making big money and that made me respectable."[57] Despite his shrinking star power and earnings, he was at peace with the tradeoffs associated with leading the fight for equality.

Gregory published *Write Me In!* in 1968. It was a semihumorous advertising tool for his campaign to win the office of president of the United States. Gregory reported that "almost one million copies" of the manifesto sold in its first year.[58] Readers got a good dose of the satirical humor that helped Gregory break new ground as an African American comedian in the early 1960s:

> People ask me, "If you were elected President, what group of people do you think you would have the most trouble with?" And I have no doubt that I would have the most trouble with colored folks. One of my first programs would be to wipe

out the poverty program and set up a 55 billion dollar a year White Folks Rest Program. I'd take all those white folks off their good jobs and put them on my Rest Program. And I'd give my black brother a good job for the first time in his life. I guarantee you that after six months of doing this, colored folks would be marching on me at the White House, saying, "What's wrong with you? Lettin' these white folk lay around not working, getting relief checks, havin' all them babies."[59]

The short book also included serious reflections on the shortcomings of American democracy and solutions to achieving a more equitable society: "When big business cheats its way to power and wealth with governmental approval, moral fallout infects the entire nation. When we wipe out the crime syndicate, we will go a long way toward eliminating crime in the streets." Gregory's challenge to entrenched systems of power eclipsed the black-white dichotomy, as he proposed a platform that would give voice to Native Americans, immigrants, and a host of other groups that he considered disenfranchised: "When all Americans are given fair and equal opportunity for growth and development, the seeds of resentment and hostility will blossom forth in the full bloom of shared citizenship."[60]

Gregory won just over 47,000 votes, less than 1 percent of the total number cast.[61] It was a noble effort, although it was met with disapproval from at least two African American leaders. Conrad Lynn, a civil rights attorney and founder of the Freedom Now party, complained that Gregory "just takes off on his own" with antics that may have been perceived by whites as stereotypical buffoonery. Whitney Young of the National Urban League believed that Gregory "could render a greater service to the civil-rights movement by continuing to reach groups as an entertainer—which none of the civil rights leaders can."[62] Lynn and Young obviously questioned the role of a comedian in the political sphere. For Lynn, Gregory's impetus to independently apply his celebrity status and resources toward campaigning for president bordered on the absurd. But Lynn failed to understand that Gregory's fearless leadership shattered conventional constraints within and beyond the arena of comedy. Young insinuated that Gregory's best usefulness resided in the entertainment realm, but he failed to grasp that Gregory could no more have limited himself to the comic stage than he could have remained still in a vehicle driving by a segregated restaurant. Gregory thrived on fighting almost any "good fight" and cared far less for protocol.

Cosby, too, disagreed with Gregory's metamorphosis from satirist to staunch activist. In March 1968, months before the presidential election, Cosby charged that the radical, combative approach to equality had defeated Gregory and another leading African American activist in the cultural arena: "Some guys, when they get in the big house, say, 'I think it stinks here,' and they rebel. What happens? What happened to Dick Gregory and Cassius Clay (Muhammad Ali)? The white man dumps all over them. Where are Gregory and Clay today? They are broke. Broke and broken."[63]

Cosby, conversely, had it all—love, fame, good health, and unimaginable wealth. *Newsweek* reported that his album sales had tripled by 1966 and that just one of his gigs at Harrah's on Lake Tahoe earned him $25,000 per week.[64] That number soon doubled to $50,000 per week and, along with his handsome checks for television, film, and other work, elevated his salary to heights to which most Americans only dreamed.[65] Cosby's tax bill in 1967 was a whopping $833,000. He devised a sly plan to create "extra" money to pay it by booking twenty-five stand-up performances during the month of January 1968. It almost worked. The quick scheme brought in $750,000.[66] By August 1968, Cosby had expanded his production company to overseas markets. Filming *I Spy* in Japan, Greece, Morocco, and other locations likely catalyzed establishment of the Campbell-Silver-Cosby Corporation (CSC) in London.

Cosby calculated each of his show business moves as part of a plan to strike it rich *and* effect racial advancement. Although he had succeeded in branding himself as the "anti–Dick Gregory," Cosby indeed wrestled with what W.E.B. Du Bois famously identified as "the problem of the color-line."[67] He viewed himself as an agent of change. "Kids ask the best questions," he once shared. "One asked me what were my goals for the Negro people. 'There's just one word,' I told him. 'Equality. Period.' "[68] Many African Americans may have questioned the authenticity of Cosby's response because of his absence from the front lines, yet his private approach to race matters reveals an individual with a genuine, progressive program.

No one activist or ideology held a monopoly on resistance. Gregory, Ali, Elaine Brown, Carmichael, and Malcolm X occupied the same "rank" in the movement as Cosby, King, John Lewis, Jo Ann Robinson, and Roy Wilkins of the NAACP. So, too, did Fannie Lou Hamer and the countless other local activists who must be considered part of the broad effort required to dismantle Jim Crow. Cosby entered the movement on his own terms and set his own goals. He desired to "change some of the beliefs and ideas that the old Hollywood established, the image of the black man."[69] Cosby wanted to take the *I Spy* formula of white and African American men coexisting without any hang-ups about race to the big screen. In 1966, he shared that he was "waiting for a producer to call and say, 'Let's make a movie where Cosby lives next to Jack Lemmon. Let's show that they're married to pretty wives and that their kids play together.'" Robert Culp fully believed that this form of activism could achieve as much as "100 marches" because of its significance in "showing what [America] could be like if there had been no hate."[70] Cosby's methods worked well among masses of whites and middle-class African Americans who sought a progressive approach to race relations devoid of the tension and controversy associated with the politics of Black Power.

Fighting against the white power structure as an "outsider" held no appeal to Cosby. For him, it was a self-defeating strategy. He preferred to work within the system to achieve a level of independence and security that enabled a "comfortable boldness." Cosby presumed that others' opinions would not matter once he had *made it*. "By 1971, the latest," he predicted, "I should be a millionaire, and when I am, I'm going to quit show business and go back to school. I want to get a degree in Phys Ed or some other thing that will allow me to work with kids."[71] A year later he echoed the same goal: "When I'm 34, goodbye. I would like to teach acting, directing and so on, to kids. That's what I really want to do. First, though, I want Bill Cosby and his wife and children to be very, very comfortable. And this is the one business I know of where that can happen."[72]

But it could not happen by following the trail laid by Gregory, who endured everything from threatening phone calls (even on the night that his infant son died) to jail sentences.[73] Cosby chose a less gritty route to reach the same end. Like most African Americans in the spotlight in the 1960s, his approach met criticism at times, but to have changed course would have indicated that he was afraid to create his own destiny. Cosby explained that his seemingly passive approach was "what you have to do in this business when you belong to the minority group. You have to walk so that you don't upset the people who are in a position to give you the next step so you can eventually walk by yourself."[74] His endgame strategy could not have been more different than Gregory's impulsive pursuits.

By any measure, Cosby's professional career through the late 1960s must be considered astoundingly successful. He eclipsed not only Gregory, but all of the veteran African American comedians and fellow newcomers who rode the tails of Gregory's earlier breakthrough. Richard Pryor had emerged and scored big by 1965, largely emulating Cosby's act. And America proved ready for Pryor's own legendary style after he reinvented himself near the end of the decade following a stint in Berkeley. In May 1968, Flip Wilson signed a five-year contract with NBC that would lead to his own series.[75] Godfrey Cambridge followed two months later with an exclusive ten-year deal with CBS.[76] But none of Cosby's contemporaries matched his success. Pryor voiced his displeasure with television sponsors' constant push for him to exhibit a "clean" persona in the vein of Cosby; he said that it called his manhood into question. "They want you to be something that really doesn't exist at all," he complained. Yet Cosby had done it masterfully. *"How did that nigger get by us?"* Pryor joked as if he were giving commentary as a white man. *"He slipped up on us with his brilliance and walked away with everything. And all we can do is go see him because we ain't got a chance in the world, can't stop him, can't hang him up . . . can't mess him up at all—nothin'—'cause he's bad!"*[77]

Cosby was "bad" because he had carefully constructed a public persona that encouraged whites to move beyond feeling comfortable with him. They felt connected. Cosby had practiced the art of "cultural passing," constructing a professional and private persona that reflected the background and sensibilities of his primary audience—the white American mainstream audience to which he played. The strategy proved so effective that many whites completely dissociated him from the race problem. By performing stand-up routines and portraying characters that were completely race neutral save for the color of his skin and participating marginally in the fight for equality, Cosby gave whites the opportunity to enjoy an African American comedian without heavy consideration of the nation's controversial race issues. More than Gregory, Ali, and Belafonte, he truly crossed over. Cosby became a wildly popular African American entertainer to whom whites in his industry and audience could attribute few, if any, upsetting comments, issues, or roles pertaining to race. The precedent he established is dangerous, as some may view simply crossing over as selling out, but evidence suggests that Cosby plotted his path to stardom with the intent of improving opportunities for African Americans as a corollary aim. Rather than selling out, he "sold up" so that he could enjoy they spoils of success and create unprecedented opportunity for African Americans and other minorities in the entertainment arena.

A 1966 *Newsweek* story captured the phenomenal degree to which Cosby mastered the art of cultural passing:

> Bill Cosby is not a Negro comic; he is a comic who happens to be a Negro. In his nightclub act, he is concerned more with dropouts than discrimination, bothered more by air pollution than prejudice. And on television, as one of two CIA men posing as tennis bums on NBC's hot new show "I Spy," his lines provide the color, not his skin.[78]

Life Magazine reached the same conclusion in its 1968 profile of the emerging comedy legend:

> His childhood is all our childhoods, with monsters in the closet, touch football in the street and fathers who keep on threatening to resort to the strap. To those who still insist on judging people by whether they are black or white, Bill Cosby may be the most subversive charmer of youth since the Pied Piper.[79]

Columnist Barbara Delatiner of *Newsday* also asserted in 1968 that "there's nothing ethnic about Bill Cosby's humor."[80] Her words provide further evidence that many whites perceived Cosby as being just like them. It was not by accident. Cosby had staked his entire career on building relationships with his largely white audiences based on their shared human experiences. He was surely pleased with the description of him as "a *human being*, and a funnier, hipper human being than anyone around him."[81] He worked hard to position himself as a comedian with cross-racial appeal. Culp identified with Cosby so greatly that he believed that "whatever you say about one of us is almost sure to be true of the other one, too." Culp was thoroughly aware of the differences in race and socioeconomic background between himself and Cosby, yet those monumental differences did not weigh as much as the perceived oneness in "attitudes and outlook" between the two.[82]

In his comedy album titled *To Russell, My Brother, Whom I Slept With*, Cosby charmed more whites into acknowledging their shared humanity with an African American man. He began with a bit about the trials of parenting, an experience unbound by race or class:

> I have two daughters. One is two. The definition of a two-year-old is any child with a right hand reach of eight feet. Man, I'm telling you, no matter what I move away from her, she can still get at it from the position she's standing in. That

arm grows and grows and grows. You ever feed a two-year-old? Two-year-olds are "ball makers." They sit down and take all the food—potatoes, string beans, and the steak—and they roll it up in a ball. All of it goes into a ball, and then they hand it to you. *"Hey, Dad. You want some?"* No, not if you don't want Dad to throw up, you don't want me to bite into that.

I have a one-year-old. She's a circle-maker with the food. Right away, picks her spoon up, no matter what it is, round and round and round and round, it goes in a circle. And a one-year-old never puts food in its mouth. They are fed by their own way, which is the "mashing method." They mash it into the—mashed potatoes, mashed and through the brain, down into the stomach. All peas and green things go in the ear, by that way. Meat goes in the neck. All milk slides down the chest and into the belly button, where it is sucked up.[83]

In 1967, *Look Magazine* reported that Cosby's race had become unnoticeable to "some 25 million mostly white Americans, southerners included." It was an exceptional breakthrough, but not everyone agreed with Cosby's disciplined participation in the fight for equality on his own terms. Some African Americans associated Cosby's apparent assimilation with accommodation, and they continued to charge that his accomplishments meant very little to the movement. Many of Cosby's detractors believed in an idea of African American masculinity that matched the rhetoric of Malcolm X, the anger of Carmichael, the leadership of King, and the visible involvement of Gregory. "He has caught some flak from civil-rights militants for not showing at freedom marches and the like," one reporter recorded. Sammy Davis Jr.—whom Gregory had chided for leaving the Meredith March before its conclusion, presumably because of the threat of violence—came to Cosby's defense: "Bill Cosby carries as much weight on his shoulders as any Negro I know. He may not be a front-runner in the cause—that's not his nature—but he's totally committed."[84]

Cosby's commitment was certainly evident in his approach to television and film work. He maintained focus on the goal of racial advancement as he carefully navigated his involvement in projects. Film offers began to pour in by 1967, and Cosby rejected those that did not meet the threshold of portraying African Americans in a positive, meaningful light. This was entirely consistent with his politics of representation, which celebrated African American men and women as equally ambitious, fun-loving, and family oriented as any other race. "Sure, everybody wants me to play 'Rastus the Slave,' or some kind of hater-junk like that," he said. "Not for me, baby. I haven't seen one [film] offer yet that would just let me be a person who holds his head up, not specifically a Negro."[85] Cosby also morphed his role on *I Spy* into a battleground in the fight for equality. After the show's first fall season, the sexual abstinence of his character, in contrast to Culp's, drew criticism from viewers as well as Cosby. "If Alexander Scott doesn't get to go out with a girl once in a while," he grumbled, "people are going to wonder about me." On the question of whether Scott could experience romance interracially—as Poitier's character did in the 1967 blockbuster *Guess Who's Coming to Dinner*—Cosby spoke as adamantly as Marcus Garvey in dismissing the possibility: "As far as white girls go, I want Scotty sterile. I believe in my women first."[86]

Depicting the image of intelligent African American men in stable relationships and families represented Cosby's attempt to counter nearly a century of stereotypes perpetuated by the entertainment industry. He hosted a CBS documentary titled *Black History: Lost, Stolen or Strayed* in 1968 that allowed him "go further" in correcting white Americans' negative attitudes toward African Americans since slavery.[87] The program featured Cosby interacting with a fourth-grade teacher, Mrs. Lovely Billups, and her integrated group of students while delivering sobering facts that ranged from Africa's "high culture" that had been repeatedly borrowed by Europeans without credit to scenes from *Guess Who's Coming to Dinner* that played into whites' expectations (African American servants loyal to their white employers) and fears (interracial relationships).[88] The connection that Cosby had established with white America qualified him as the perfect messenger. The program came across as more educational than racial, especially considering the backdrop of the integrated classroom. Cosby's race-neutral persona made him well positioned as an ambassador to white America who could usher a television special on African American history into the mainstream. Cosby delivered his lessons with a cordial and occasionally funny presence that perhaps no other African American entertainer could have matched.

At no point in the documentary did Cosby demonstrate the intensity of Gregory or Carmichael, but his ideas reflected Black Power aims. While presenting an image of an African man being publicly bathed by whites in the early nineteenth century, Cosby addressed the symbolism in an entirely nonthreatening tone:

> Take the Lewis and Clarke expedition; you'll find a black man named York, helping to open the West. Those men are trying to wash the black out of York. That's what you might call historically significant because a lot of people think we ought to wash white, but we ain't gonna.

Regarding one of America's most popular presidents, he continued to subtly plant seeds of African American equality:

> How about Teddy Roosevelt's charge up San Juan Hill? It wasn't just the Rough Riders who made it. Four black regiments went right up with Teddy. They didn't get lost going up the hill. They got lost in the history books.

Cosby later spoke words that provide insight to his criteria for determining whether to entertain particular television or film offers. His comments reflected ideas presented in the 1965 Moynihan Report, a study conducted by the U.S. Department of Labor that traced the psychological legacy of slavery and oppression on African American families:

> America invented the cruelest history in the world because it broke up black families. After slavery was over, America kept breaking up the black man's family. And that's some awful history to teach. Now, if you want to look history right straight in the eye, you're going to get a black eye, because it isn't important whether a few black heroes got lost or stolen or strayed in America's history textbooks. What's important is *why* they got left out.

Few in the 1960s were aware of the degree to which Cosby aggressively negotiated the African American image in society and popular culture. His refusal to accept roles that would have made "a lot of people, mostly black, sick to their stomach" dealt an important strike in favor of the movement.[89] His insistence on *I Spy's* Alexander Scott dating black women affirmed African American manhood *and* the beauty of African American women. Not only did Cosby's calculated contributions mirror the era's more visible activists in principle, but they also freed many whites to adopt new attitudes that recognized the equal humanity of African Americans. His cultural activism produced gains that were unmeasured, unrecognized, and underappreciated by his contemporaries. He had become a Black *Cultural* Power activist—but his master plan would not truly unfold until he "walked by himself" with full control of the Cosby brand.

Chapter 5

Edutainment

In the late 1960s and early 1970s, Gregory called for increased agitation against civil and human rights abuses. His public identity became that of an inflamed radical. Gregory traveled to Paris in 1969 to meet with leaders from North Vietnam, the nation that America had engaged in war. A. Donald Bourgeois, an African American attorney well connected to the power establishment in Chicago, accompanied Gregory on the trip as "a friend and confidant." He described his friend Dick as a " 'lone wolf' civil and peace rights advocate who often has been criticized by civil rights and peace groups for refusing to join them."[1] The description was accurate. Gregory impressively championed a plethora of civil and human rights issues, but he upset many by developing a personal philosophy of rabid activism through which he declared friends, enemies, and strategies on his own terms. By the end of the 1960s, his habit of standing alone alienated some potential comrades and media supporters. The broad strokes Gregory painted as the Civil Rights Movement entered a new decade lacked the humor evident in his comedic beginnings.

By contrast, Bill Cosby's path in the late 1960s and early 1970s led to heights previously unimaginable for African American comedians. He transcended the traditional boundaries of stand-up gigs and television appearances by adding song albums, motion pictures, and pitch work for commercial products to his brand. The creative license that Cosby carved out for himself appeared limitless. He proved capable of carrying television programs almost as a one-man show, and networks demonstrated a willingness to give him full control of casting and production. "There are few performers today who can fill almost an entire hour with monologues," but "Mr. Cosby did just that and with a warm humor that was unfailingly contagious." Mainstream America's love fest with the comedian uniquely positioned him to make political statements on his own terms: "in his own way Mr. Cosby puts the cause of integration in a winning dimension."[2]

With a strict politics of representation devoid of militancy and agitation in the public sphere, no endeavor seemed beyond Cosby's reach. In 1977, he became *Dr.* Cosby, giving him the impressive distinction of having reached the pinnacle of success in two fields—entertainment and education. Even Gregory suggested that Cosby's representation as a respectable African American entertainment celebrity deserved greater influence than his own protest activities within the struggle for African American freedom.

On March 6, 1969, Gregory recorded a four-sided album titled *Dick Gregory: The Light Side: The Dark Side*. It won immediate praise for its powerful commentary on human rights, democratic capitalism, and racism in America. The album captured a lecture that Gregory delivered on the campus of Southampton College in Long Island, New York. He pulled no punches, making his audience of predominantly white college students aware of the "moral pollution" that plagued the nation as well as their duty to fix it. "You're responsible for this white racist system," Gregory charged. "Not that you *are* a racist, [but] you're responsible for the system because it's yours."[3] His intensity remained high throughout the recording, and his delivery differed immensely from his earlier albums. Gregory spoke with passion and, at times, anger. Following a brief introductory anecdote, Gregory's serious discussion of hot-button topics elicited far less laughter than his earlier stand-up recordings.

The Light Side: The Dark Side was recorded less than a year after protests in several major cities occurred following the assassination of Martin Luther King Jr. The death toll in Chicago reached eleven within days, and the arsons and lootings left more than 1,000 African Americans jailed or detained.[4] Mayor Richard Daley issued a personal plea for all Chicagoans to "protect the city and work and cooperate with police, the Illinois national guard, and the fine fire department."[5] Daley also ordered that law enforcement "shoot to kill arsonists and 'shoot to maim or cripple' looters," which Gregory sternly condemned early in his address at Southampton:

> The fact that we emphasize property rights is the reason Mayor Daley of Chicago made that statement he made—*shoot all*

looters to kill. Never said shoot murderers to kill [or] shoot dope pushers to kill. You know why? Because murderers and dope pushers deal with the human right, looters deal with property. And, to be honest with you, when Mayor Daley made that statement pertaining to shooting all looters to kill, it's the first time I ever agreed with him. Yeah, I hurried up and sent him a telegram. I said, *Dear Fool, Your statement pertaining to shooting all looters to kill, I agree with wholeheartedly if you make one stipulation. Let's first make it retroactive and let's first put the gun in the Indians' hand.*[6]

The crowd was silent. The Reverend Jesse Jackson had decried Mayor Daley's directive as "a fascist response," and other African American leaders had expressed their dismay.[7] Gregory's angle fell in line with the pulse of many African Americans; nevertheless, it shocked most in the audience.

The students heard more of Gregory's frustrations with American race relations along with his extreme remedies for improvement. He condemned the demeaning practice, particularly in the South, of whites referring to African Americans by their first names—or simply "boy" and "girl"—while African Americans called whites "mister," "miss," "sir," and "ma'am." Gregory identified the social inequality of the decades-long practice designed to elevate the status of whites and cement the inferiority of blacks.[8] He attacked the ongoing power differential in interracial communication and shared the lengths to which he and his wife, Lillian, went to ensure that their newborn daughter would be addressed respectfully:

When my last baby daughter that was born six months ago— we know how the system hates to call black folks "Mr." and "Mrs.," so we named her M-I-S-S. That's her first name—*Miss.* Last name is Gregory. Anybody wanna talk to her will have to call her *Miss* Gregory.

It was not a joke. Miss Gregory had been born on October 17, 1968. Gregory and his wife prepared Miss and her siblings for the language of racism that they were likely to encounter:

I remember when I was a kid. My mother, my father, my whole community taught me *"one day you're going to grow up, boy, and a white man is going to call you a nigger. And don't get mad 'cause God don't like no ugly."* Sure enough, I grew up, and a cracker called me a nigger, and I didn't get mad neither, *'cause God don't like no ugly.* You know, I got seven little black kids at home right now, and me and my old lady ain't teaching them *nothing*.

The abuses of American business and government provided a strong underlying theme in Gregory's approximately ninety-minute lecture. He challenged youth to "move the capitalists behind the United States Constitution" using the power of the boycott, which would produce swift results if managed appropriately. Gregory suggested the recording and cattle industries as excellent targets. He counseled those in attendance who wished for educational reform to forego taking over administration buildings in favor of boycotting meat consumption five days per week: the right-wing, wealthy cattle growers would "fly into town and kick the doors off the president's office" in support of their demands, he predicted. Gregory also dared Southampton youth to question and, when necessary, rebel against the establishment:

> One question you got to ask loud and clear—it's a simple question. That question is, if democracy is as good as we tell you it is, then why in the hell are we running all over the world trying to ram it down people's throat with a gun? The day you youngsters work to make this democracy work right for the first time, that's the day we can bring the guns home. Because, you see, anything good you don't have to force on people. They will steal it.[9]

Gregory knew that *The Light Side: The Dark Side* was something special. He watched it grow as "one of the big hits on the charts" and viewed it as "probably one of the most important works I've ever done in my life."[10] *New York Times* journalist Lindsay Patterson suggested that March 6 "should be declared a national holiday." She considered the fiery work a "masterpiece" full of ideas that had been ignored by white America for too long. "If I could have one demand turned into law," Patterson wrote, "it would be this: That every white American, from the President on down, be compelled to listen to it again and again and again. And not simply just to listen either, but to absorb the album's message, which is contained in the most lucid, forceful and witty discourse about racism in America yet on record."[11]

National Educational Television (NET) subsequently taped Gregory giving his "Light Side, Dark Side" address to students at the University of Alabama in Tuscaloosa and aired the program on January 5, 1970. It was marketed as a "remarkable mixture of bitterness, humor, wisdom and satire" that would move viewers to "laughter, tears, rage or thoughtfulness."[12] The *New York Times* applauded NET for "keeping the airwaves open to stimulating dialogue," although the one-hour production did not go entirely as planned.[13] A "power failure" in northwest Chicago blacked out the program after thirty-seven minutes. Hundreds of unhappy viewers called in protest. Carol Bryant, publicity director for the television station, said that "many callers had voiced suspicions that Mayor Richard J. Daley [sic] might have had something to do with the power failure."[14] Another station representative said that some callers thought the station pulled the plug on the show because "Gregory was getting too hot."[15] The station issued an apology and announced plans to re-air the program. Although Gregory had no direct role in the controversy, it bolstered his reputation as an independent radical taking on the white American establishment.

Across the Atlantic, African nations' anticolonial movements shaped and borrowed from the struggle for freedom in America. Since the Berlin Conference of 1885, when several European nations began partitioning Africa into colonial territories, African political, social, and economic systems experienced widespread destruction. European nations exploited the continent. The scene was all too familiar to African Americans: a white power structure that demonstrated little regard for millions of black bodies, a social order that pitted whites over Africans, and consistent pleas by the underclass for freedom and equality.[16]

The struggle for freedom on both sides of the Atlantic helped establish meaningful communications between African Americans and continental Africans. Kwame Nimako argues that Ghana's first prime minister in its postcolonial era, Kwame Nkrumah, "was awakened by Black America and [that] he in turn awakened Black America."[17] Nkrumah was born in Ghana but spent several years studying in the United States. The teachings of Marcus Garvey proved influential to his political program upon his return to West Africa, as he revealed in his autobiography that "of all the literature I studied, the book that did more than any other to fire my enthusiasm was *The Philosophy and Opinions of Marcus Garvey*."[18] Nkrumah decorated his new government with the symbolism of Garvey's Black Star and the rhetoric of freedom, which, according to Nimako, "was also taken from Black America." His elevation of Kente cloth to "the level of a national dress code" traveled across the Atlantic and helped shape African Americans' expressions of their African heritage. Oppression bonded millions of African descendants who had been geographically separated for generations. Nkrumah charged that "the same power structure which is blocking the efforts of African-Americans in the US is also now throwing road-blocks in Africa's way."[19]

Nkrumah led Ghana from its independence from the British in 1957 until his coup in 1966. His leadership overlapped with the height of the struggle for African American freedom, and his connection to the United States positioned Ghana as the movement's West African hub. Dozens of well-known African Americans and a greater number of lesser-known individuals traveled to Ghana and other African countries in the 1960s and 1970s to demonstrate their pride and solidarity. Richard Wright, W.E.B. Du Bois, A. Philip Randolph, Ralph Bunche, Maya Angelou, Martin Luther King Jr., and Adam Clayton Powell Jr. all joined in the "hope that the brilliant example of Ghana will spur [African Americans] to close ranks similarly and pool our talents and resources so that we in the great American democracy may attain a larger measure of independence."[20]

Gregory made his first trip to Africa in 1970. He joined activists from across the world at the Conference of Nonaligned Third World Nations in Lusaka, Zambia, to speak against colonialism and imperialism.[21] His visit indicated that he located the struggle for African American freedom as part of an international movement against oppression. Gregory stopped along the way in Kenya, which, like Ghana and Zambia, had recently wrestled itself free from several decades of colonization by the British. Seeing the motherland was such a moving experience that he made separate arrangements for two of his children, eleven-year-old Michelle and nine-year-old Lynne, to also visit. *Jet Magazine* announced that Michelle and Lynne had embarked on a journey "to learn more about the Mother Country" and would spend time in Ivory Coast, Ghana, Nigeria, Liberia and Senegal. Dr. Leonard Jeffries, a college professor at San Jose State College, where Gregory had previously lectured for six weeks, organized the trip.[22] Gregory sent these young children on a trip abroad unaccompanied by either parent, as Lillian was very close to delivering their eighth child. Gregory stated: "Every Black person in America should go home at least once in his or her lifetime."[23]

Speaking at anti–Vietnam War protests on the continent of Australia had been part of Gregory's extended travel plan, but the Australian government denied him entry upon his landing. Immigration Minister Philip Lynch explained to Parliament that "the reason given in his visa application (sightseeing) is not bona fide, not genuine and is spurious in intent."[24] Gregory was furious, and he blamed the CIA for blocking his interaction with Australian people, particularly college students. "Thanks to the CIA," he charged, "the Australian government believed our visit would be disruptive. It was no secret that I was opposed to the Vietnam War; I talked about it everywhere I went. Based on my antiwar sentiment and the fact that Australia had fighting forces in Vietnam, they refused to issue us visas."[25] The *New York Amsterdam News* suggested racism as one of the factors behind Gregory's forced turnaround: "it is known that 'the land down under' has never encouraged blacks to either visit or live in that country."[26] Australian journalist Maximilian Walsh asserted that race *and* politics were to blame, as the conservative prime minister had been working to make "law and order" an issue in upcoming elections. Gregory, a high-profile "black agitator" in a country "where racism is not far below the surface in many areas," provided an excellent opportunity for the government to publicize its agenda.[27] He voiced his frustration while meeting with the news media in Nairobi, Kenya: "It's confusing as hell. Here in Africa I meet people who are earnestly trying to build nations, and elsewhere nations are trying to destroy themselves."[28]

Gregory had seen a lot of physical and psychological damage inflicted by governments against African descendants and other non-white peoples worldwide. He considered nations that abused its citizens morally bankrupt. In the United States, he had lived through the assassinations of John F. Kennedy, Malcolm X, Martin Luther King Jr., and Robert Kennedy, all of whom he believed fell because of the workings of a CIA that Americans "don't know enough about."[29] Gregory believed that the organization had tapped his phone and placed him under surveillance. It was a form of terror consistent with other government-sponsored activities that matched the United Nations definition of genocide. In November 1970, he joined actor Ossie Davis in leading a coalition of African Americans and Puerto Ricans in asking the United Nations to censure the United States. "The whole world is aware of our policies here," Gregory said.[30] Davis hoped to see the United Nations "condemn the United States and impose sanctions" as it had done with South Africa based on its policy of apartheid.[31]

Gregory's involvement with the petition served as another passionate outpouring of his commitment to justice, which had become far less calculated than it had been in the early 1960s. It was indicative, as he said, of having "graduated from the civil-rights movement to the human-rights movement." Furthermore, the Gregory of the late 1960s and early 1970s doubted the usefulness of humor as a political tool, possibly because he operated so close to the front lines that it proved difficult for him to see the larger effectiveness of his work: "You know we didn't laugh Hitler out of existence," he said, "and there will be a cure found for cancer, only it won't be good humor." His name recognition and independence allowed him to insert himself into human rights issues, from Native American fishing rights to poverty and oppression in Europe and Africa. Gregory's scattered activities and unpredictable methods certainly would not have been endorsed by any established civil rights organization, and the mainstream audience did not respond to his transition from "impertinent stand-up comic to serious social activist" enthusiastically. "Without doubt," Richard M. Williams wrote, "much of white America does not relish the change."[32]

While stirrings of Gregory's change were evident by the mid-1960s, his noncomedic agenda developed fully in the late 1960s and early 1970s. He penned an editorial for the *New York Times* in 1969 that explained his retreat from the entertainment realm. African American artists had been "called upon" not to disengage from their crafts, necessarily, but to prevent their talents from supporting industries, such as television and film, that were "thoroughly infected with the disease of racism." They needed to pressure the entertainment industry to rid itself of racial stereotypes. "We don't have any more Amos 'n' Andys, or Stepin Fetchits, or Mantan Morelands, perpetrating a myth," Gregory declared. He hoped to see more African American artists committed to rejecting such portrayals and destroying racist attitudes rather than losing themselves in the "*exclusive* pursuit of a career."[33]

One of the entertainers whom Gregory named as demonstrative of the appropriate way to pursue a career in entertainment while maintaining a socially progressive politics of representation was Cosby. "Bill Cosby may be the most significant thing that ever happened for black folks and he doesn't even know it," Gregory said. "Now, my kids can see him every week and identify with him. White folks can see him, too, and see a black man who isn't in a jail scene or Commie rally."[34] It was a genuine compliment. Gregory endorsed Cosby as a fellow crusader in the struggle for African American freedom, even though Cosby's voice on race matters remained so consistently silent that Gregory presumed Cosby might not have known his own value. Gregory viewed Cosby as an equal, if not superior, influence. He told *Newsweek* that "it's more important for my children to see a black face on the TV screen than in a demonstration."[35]

In acknowledging Cosby's meaningful place in the struggle, Gregory communicated his understanding of the broad effort required to combat white supremacy. He believed that Malcolm X and Martin Luther King Jr. had been complementary forces, and similarly located Cosby as his important counterpart in the movement. But Gregory now adhered to a "moral imperative" that distinguished him from Cosby and other entertainers.[36] He made surprising career moves and centered himself in controversies because he believed it to be the right thing to do. Martin Luther King Jr. had once said that "injustice anywhere is a threat to justice everywhere."[37] Gregory internalized the idea. In the late 1960s and early 1970s, he extended his stage beyond clubs and late-night television shows. He wanted to make sure that the next generation of white leaders and policy makers in America—college students—heard "the truth" and understood their role in ensuring civil and human rights for all.

The evolution of Gregory amounted to a near complete change of audience by 1970. He began to spend "about 98 percent of his time" with college youth upon whom the "fate and destiny of America depends."[38] Gregory believed that the nation's millions of youth were eager to usher in a new era and that they had been "crying out for direction." He shared the rebel spirit of white America's counterculture and joined many other radical speakers in visiting the nation's colleges. Serving as a sounding board to restless white youth became an important part of Gregory's new program. Following his campus lectures, Gregory commonly spent hours facilitating informal discussions with those who had further questions and comments. A *Hartford Times* article reported that college students "have gobbled it up."[39] Gregory's travel schedule reflected the success of his modified activism. In one eight-month span, he spent approximately $35,000 on plane fare.[40] He later estimated that he spoke at "three hundred colleges a year, sometimes two per day."[41] Students' increased participation in civic affairs both satisfied and energized Gregory. He seemed hopeful that "young white kids" had embraced the movement. "Even the Chinese kids in California have got a movement," he said.[42] He thanked them for moving America for the first time into "talking about the Indian and the black and the Chicano [and] about poor white folks in Appalachia and about the Asian-American."[43]

Gregory's new direction in human rights leadership paid some dividends. According to one report, his emergence on the college speaker circuit enabled him to make "upwards of $300,000 a year while entertaining more than a million people."[44] *Ebony* suggested that his demand on college campuses generated income of $500,000 a year, and further posited that "publishing royalties bring him an estimated $250,000 per book."[45] But Gregory valued the movement more than money. "I probably could be the most well paid [college speaker] if I wanted to," he said. "I could go for three to five thousand dollars per lecture." However, he purposely kept his speaking fee between $1,000 and $1,500 so that smaller colleges could afford to book him.[46]

While Gregory's annual salary returned to its heights, it did not amount to the most comfortable of lifestyles. He had become more deeply involved as an activist, and contributed dollar amounts to the movement that eclipsed his giving in the early 1960s. The $100,000 advance he received for *Write Me In!* served as the primary funding source for his presidential campaign. His cost to attend conferences, meetings, and rallies approached the six-figure mark annually, which was in addition to the money that he sacrificed by placing a cap on his speaking fee. Gregory had splurged shortly after becoming a mainstream success in the early 1960s based on a humorous and interesting rationale: "I think to be born black or poor white in America, you owe yourself two hundred thousand dollars worth of treats just to un-mess up your mind," he said.[47] But by the early 1970s, Gregory had little interest in purchasing top-of-the-line luxuries, such as the Rolls-Royce that he once owned and lost by repossession (as his children clapped because they found the spectacle entertaining). He bought a farm in Plymouth, Massachusetts, but his major expenditures remained within the movement. During the months that college students enjoyed summer break, Gregory returned to stand-up comedy to supplement his income. He earned approximately $10,000 per week for the infrequent gigs. When a reporter asked if he was working the club scene during the summer months because he needed the money, he answered, "Not necessarily. I'm as broke as I always been."[48]

Gregory had long taken issue with the culture of white-owned nightclubs. To ensure that African American patrons received equal treatment, he anonymously gifted tickets and large amounts of cash to prospective show attendees. If they reported discrimination when Gregory later contacted them, then he raised the issue with respective club owners. Unlike other

African American comedians, he transformed single, local performances into direct action campaigns.

Healthy living became a central component of Gregory's modified program by 1970. "He quit cigarettes and alcohol," which helped him drop pounds "by the score," and he grew to oppose working in establishments that permitted or sold either.[49] "There was a time when Gregory would consume a fifth of alcohol a day," *Newsweek* reported. "Today, he leads the Spartan existence of a health-food addict, eating only fruits, nuts and vegetables."[50] The latter disappeared from his diet by 1972. "I'm a fruitarian," Gregory proclaimed. "I haven't eaten vegetables in two years."[51]

Fasting provided him with a new method of protest. He stopped eating solid food in 1968 in protest of the war in Vietnam, and he then applied the tactic in advocacy of other major issues. It represented the "number one most mighty weapon in the non-violent arsenal," he believed, and could be used to "create a rallying point where all the honest, ethical forces can gather."[52] While imprisoned for standing with Native Americans in Washington to protect their fishing rights, Gregory "was offered food at every meal during his 40 days in jail but insisted on only taking distilled water." He was released and hospitalized after his weight dropped from 160 to 135 pounds.[53] Gregory announced a forty-day fast in June of 1970 with the expectation that greater awareness of America's serious drug problem would spread among the country's youth. "I hope," he explained, "they will realize that the same system which keeps 18-year-olds from voting, allows 18-year-olds to get dope any time they want it."[54]

By 1972, Gregory's "fruitarian" lifestyle and hunger strikes cut his weight down to ninety-eight pounds, far below the 250-plus pounds he weighed in the earlier 1960s. "Yet there is nothing ascetic or suffering in his looks, and his wit is as quick and sharp as ever," an interviewer noted.[55] Gregory addressed concerns about his well-being, arguing that people need not worry: "I'm thin but I'm healthy. Besides, if they don't end the Vietnam War soon, I'm gonna call a press conference myself and announce that the war is over."[56] His nutritional choices and weight loss positioned him for a new type of book project. *Dick Gregory's Natural Diet for Folks Who Eat: Cookin' with Mother Nature* landed on shelves in 1973. The *New York Times* called it "good fun and a good guide for those who feel they are what they eat."[57] Lesley Crosson, reviewer for the *New York Amsterdam News*, raved about Gregory's ability to provide entertainment in a healthy living guide. She credited him for making her "want to read something that contradicted every attitude I ever had about eating." She asked, rhetorically, "if Dick Gregory is going to be so reasonable about the necessity of nourishing your body instead of just feeding it, why can't he, at least, be boring?"[58]

In December 1973, Gregory announced plans to relocate his family from Illinois to Massachusetts. Thousands of Chicagoans felt the loss of one of the city's most recognized personalities. The Chicago Society of Writers and Editors (WE) organized a farewell salute to "confer the appropriate honor on Gregory for his contributions to the civil and human rights movement and his crusading efforts to help make Chicago a better place."[59] But the Gregory who left Chicago was "more caustic than the Gregory of 1960, whose bag of tricks held more wit than anger." A reporter offered possible reasons for his dramatic turn: "A hardening of the laugh glands, perhaps? Or a reflection of the political murders which have reddened so many pages of our history?"[60] The star-studded event attracted a guest list that included television host Ed Sullivan, musicians Duke Ellington and Al Green, actors Ruby Dee and Ossie Davis, Illinois Senator Richard Newhouse, comedian Godfrey Cambridge, PUSH founder Jesse Jackson, representatives from the League of Black Women, and thousands more. Al Duckett, founder of WE, remarked that "it would just basically be bad manners—if not downright ingratitude to allow Dick Gregory to leave Chicago without our city's saying 'So long but not good bye' and 'thanks for all [that] this sacrificing, spiritual man has done for civil and human rights in our town, nation and throughout the world.'"[61] It was a well-deserved moment for Gregory. For more than a decade, he had given selflessly as a leading contributor to one of America's greatest movements.

Gregory also retired from stand-up comedy in 1973. By this time, he was more of an activist than an entertainer. "As a comedian, he seemed to be a has-been because he had immersed himself so deeply in the civil-rights movement that he rarely had time to perform," one journalist recorded.[62] As early as 1969, appearing with James Baldwin at a meeting with West Indian students in London, Gregory spoke of his entertainment career in the past tense. He never lost his wit or ability to completely engage a large audience, but had certainly taken on the responsibility of improving humanity through measures beyond the arena of comedy.

The plight of the hungry across the world concerned Gregory. In 1974, he embarked on a cross-country run from Chicago to Washington, DC, designed to highlight his "war against poverty and hunger."[63] He tested his personally developed nutritional drink—Formula Four X—along the way, a product that would later be commercialized and endorsed by Muhammad Ali.[64] Gregory offered a moving explanation for his motivation to carry the struggle of so many desperate and impoverished human beings:

> I thought about Momma as I ran from city to city, state to state. Sometimes I would run all day without seeing a tree, a house, or even a bird, just open lonely highways. I wondered if she could see me on those lonely roads. Almost all of her life, Momma had walked the streets of St. Louis trying to feed her babies. There I was, twenty-two years later, running across America for all the poor children like me. I understood the sound of hunger coming from their little stomachs; I understood Momma.
>
> It was the thought of Momma and all those nights that we went to bed hungry that made me keep running. I ran in hopes that no other child would have to go through what my brothers and sisters and I had gone through. I just kept running and praying—I couldn't give up even if I wanted to. King had been dead for six years, and a part of the Movement died with him. Many poor people just gave up. I wanted people to know we were still fighting for them; I wanted them to know that they were not forgotten and that they were not alone.[65]

Gregory's impassioned and multidirectional crusading made it difficult for mainstream America to readily identify with him. Although his independence allowed him the freedom to determine his own agenda, it diluted his brand. Would-be supporters moved away from Gregory because he failed to consolidate his energies and methods into one easily digestible package. His ideas and activities proved too unpredictable to be grasped.

Meanwhile, Cosby's consistency and familiarity struck the right chord. His avoidance of political issues in the public sphere helped him become the most successful African American comedic figure in the nation. Cosby once told a reporter about white people who spoke openly to him about race: "People say to me, 'I don't think of you as a Negro.'" Cosby understood the message to mean that he was not viewed as "a problem."[66] Compared with Gregory and several other outspoken movement leaders who advocated for "freedom now" against the backdrop of Black Power, Cosby gave whites the ability to dissociate him from the movement, just as many of them had dissociated him from race.

In 1969, NBC rewarded Cosby's talent and cross-racial appeal by providing him full license to create and star in his own weekly television series. It was a gamble for the network despite Cosby's immense popularity. *The Sammy Davis, Jr. Show* had lasted just four months on NBC in 1966 before being canceled. *Julia*, a 1968 television series starring African American actress Diahann Caroll, fared much better, but only temporarily. Carroll starred in the role of Julia Baker, a nurse and widowed mother of a six-year-old son. The most controversial aspect of the show was its failure to portray any of the harsher realities of African American life, particularly in urban ghettos.[67] *Julia* completely avoided racial issues, which invited criticism for a lack of realism from African Americans. Carroll initially defended her role on the show: "Because I am black, that doesn't mean that I have to deal with the problems of all black people," she said. "That's not my sole responsibility."[68] However, she soon echoed the criticisms of many whites who believed that the show's white writers proved patronizing to African Americans. Carroll believed that they were "presenting the white Negro [who] has very little Negro-ness."[69] The formula proved successful enough to register *Julia* as the seventh most popular program in 1968–69, its first season. But it fell to twenty-eighth in 1969–70, the same season that NBC invested deeply in the magic of Cosby, and Carroll soon asked for her release.[70]

The Bill Cosby Show represented Cosby's first opportunity for total creative control of his work since his earliest stand-up comedy performances. Along with agent Roy Silver and producer Bruce Campbell, Cosby had become a third of the Campbell, Silver and Cosby Corporation (CS&C) in 1967, which carefully managed his blossoming television career. CS&C had possibly joined NBC in suggesting that Cosby's new television program feature him as a police detective. The idea did not match Cosby's vision, and his establishment of Jemmin, Inc.—named after Cosby's grandfather, "who used to say 'Jemmin' when he was trying to say 'gentlemen' "—meant that the comedian and actor claimed sole authority over his career.[71] The breakup between Cosby and his partners was bitter. "I no longer have anything to do with them," he told *Jet* in 1969.[72] "I have a right to approval," he later explained with a "tinge of acid" in his voice. The comment suggested that Campbell and Silver disagreed with several of his ideas prior to *The Bill Cosby Show*. Writer Kay Gardella noted that "the bitterness the comic still feels for his associates cannot be hid."[73] Cosby had hinted at operating independently earlier in his career, although he realized the level of success required for an African American comedian to attempt such a move. But by 1969, the multimillionaire Cosby sat atop the field of *all* American comedians and carried enough star power to favorably negotiate nearly any project. He relished the freedom that came with his new role as executive producer with Jemmin, Inc.

The discord between Cosby and his former partners ran deeper than creative differences. Cosby and Silver had punched it out early in the comedian's career when he failed to remove racial humor from his act, as the two had agreed upon. The extent to which *The Bill Cosby Show* would reflect Cosby's proposed representation of an African American man in the late 1960s may very well have been their final disagreement. The recommendation that the weekly series be based on a main character who worked in law enforcement promised success, as it would continue Cosby's race-neutral action character from *I Spy*. It made sense. However, Cosby had grown to favor a more *human* representation of people, particularly African Americans. "The good guys you see on television to me are guys who are not real," he said. "You've got to see the real character." Cosby envisioned himself playing the role of a schoolteacher at an integrated high school, more of an average man than a hero. "Bring out the good and the bad," he said, "and let people at home view it through an X-ray machine so that they can see inside him, so that they see he's not a perfect human being." Cosby's prescription for the role ran counter to his charming character on *I Spy*. Viewers would see more of themselves in Cosby's new character, especially because Cosby wanted the character to have friends of the opposite sex. Unlike the role he portrayed on *I Spy*, Cosby struck out on his own to create a character who would "also have a mother and a father, an older brother and a sister-in-law."[74] The fuller character stood to promote greater understanding of African Americans' struggles, ambitions, interpersonal relationships, and common humanity.

Chet Kincaid, the main character on *The Bill Cosby Show*, projected Cosby's idea of a working-class African American man. "He makes mistakes, gets into trouble and reflects quite frequently the human condition," Cosby said. Kincaid's daily life appealed to African American viewers who may not have identified as easily with Alexander Scott, a multilingual international spy who operated exclusively in a white world. Middle-class African Americans might more easily support Cosby's traditional politics of representation, but many poor and working-class African Americans responded critically to his perceived race neutrality. Now, as the most influential voice behind the direction of *The Bill Cosby Show*, Cosby crafted a working-class plot and cast of characters who spoke to many who may not have seen much of themselves in his earlier work. Aside from Sidney Poitier, perhaps no other African American entertainer could have rejected the push to make his or her character a private detective, but Cosby had earned the leverage to "make Chet Kincaid do anything I want him to do."75

The Bill Cosby Show premiered on September 14, 1969. Episode one followed Kincaid, a physical education teacher, on his day off. The program's "mild" debut set off few sparks in the television world, prompting Ronald Smith to note that "about the most exciting thing that happened was that a pair of cops pulled [Kincaid] over while he was jogging, thinking he might be a neighborhood prowler."76 Although critics may have wished for more fast-paced action or situations that depicted the intensity of America's race problem, the episode reflected Cosby's intentions quite well. Similar to his stand-up routines, he had designed a television series about a fairly ordinary African American man with relatable humanism. Neither exotic plots nor controversial race matters fit into Cosby's imagination, as his style called for a subtler approach to the obvious. His successful career had been a testament to the philosophy that "hitting people over the head with racial issues won't change anybody's mind."77

The criticism that Cosby predicted soon appeared. Faith Berry, an African American woman, wrote a scathing article in the *New York Times* that condemned *The Bill Cosby Show* for failing to deliver a more politically charged representation of African American life. Berry admitted that she should not have been surprised. "Unlike Dick Gregory," she said, "Cosby didn't have a reputation for putting his career on the line to tell it like it is." For Berry, Cosby's new show proved guilty of feeding the same stereotype of African American men that his role on *I Spy* projected—that of a "useful tool, the cooperative, all-too-often flunky accomplice made to look heroic." She charged that *The Bill Cosby Show* presented a fantasy because of Kincaid's friendships and acceptance in white spaces, "fairly sexless life," and apparent disinterest in race and labor issues. It appeared too unrealistic that Kincaid was "everybody's friend, usually all the time." Berry acknowledged that the program provided more opportunities for African American actors than any prior or competing television series, and that its first episode included a brief consideration of racial profiling. But neither diverted her attack. Even the scene in which Kincaid was stopped while jogging because he fit the description of a robber could have been replaced with "something more worthwhile." Berry thought that Cosby was playing the same kind of character, "that of a half-man who, had he lived during the days of Nat Turner, might have sold Turner down the river."78

Cosby's practice of carefully guarding his public comments invited critics such as Berry to overlook his character's complexity. While working on the first season of *The Bill Cosby Show*, he addressed the perpetual questioning of his status as an African American celebrity with political capital: "I help black people in my own way," he said. "It's just that I don't talk about it."[79] Cosby's way amounted to subtle but significant advances, creating the license to call his own shots. A. S. "Doc" Young noted that he "opened the doors of opportunity for black professionals, artisans and apprentices who previously were denied entrance to major network TV and to Hollywood studios." Cosby's contract with NBC stipulated an integrated production crew, including Asians and Mexicans. In this regard, he closely mirrored the demands that Gregory once placed on nightclub owners to hire African Americans on their waitstaff. Cosby's moves reflected that he had become a power broker in the entertainment industry. According to Young, "his strength and his self-sufficiency enable him to make the invaluable contribution to the cause—and to the nation—that he is making."[80]

Yet Cosby's popularity with mainstream America depended on him maintaining a fairly conservative politics of representation. Adopting the "new black image" of the late 1960s and early 1970s, which called for heightened militancy and resistance, would certainly have diminished his brand, although it would have won over many working-class African Americans. Young insightfully argued that "no one would benefit, but many would be hurt, if Cosby dashed into a television studio and told it like many of his critics say it is, which really is the essence of the matter, and blew himself right off TV because the [white] public didn't dig him." Cosby had no room to demonstrate the outspokenness of Gregory or Ali even if the desire had been present. "Bill Cosby is not Malcolm X or Dr. Martin Luther King, Eldridge Cleaver or Stokely Carmichael," Young explained. "Bill Cosby is Bill Cosby, and he is something special."[81] It was not that easy for one of the staunchest critics of *The Bill Cosby Show* to comprehend. "Many white viewers will continue to watch it because they find it refreshing," Berry concluded.[82] Her comment took a shot at Cosby's conscious avoidance of race matters, and it proved true. *The Bill Cosby Show* made an impressive eleventh-place finish in its first season.

Cosby shocked NBC executives by announcing his decision to leave *The Bill Cosby Show* in its second season to complete doctoral study in the field of education. Those in Cosby's inner circle likely took the announcement in stride. His narration of a documentary titled *Give Us the Children* in May 1970 may have heightened his urgency to contribute to uplifting youth through education. The documentary earned praise for its "avoidance of a passive stance, opting instead for a positive 'look what can be done' approach." Cosby won credit for being "invaluable as a persuasive spokesman" for the mission to improve the quality of instruction in failing schools.[83] His transformation from high school dropout to educated, upwardly mobile adult was an experience that he longed to share with American youth. Cosby aimed to motivate them to reach their full potential, just as his experiences in the Navy and college had unlocked his. His educational program would target students before they grew disenchanted with school systems that failed to reach them.

CBS executives understood and accommodated his goals. "Bill Cosby has a total commitment to education," the network announced after it lured him from NBC. "Fortunately for us, he realizes that television offers an ideal medium for narrowing the gap between education and entertainment, which is why he agreed to a major commitment to CBS."[84] *The New Bill Cosby Show*, a short-lived variety television program, emerged in 1972 alongside the comedian's plans to begin doctoral study at the University of Massachusetts.

Educating the masses directed Cosby's activities after leaving NBC. He expanded his fan base to include children and teenagers by developing G-rated programs. *Fat Albert and His Friends*, a television special that communicated life lessons through the experiences of a group of African American adolescent friends in Philadelphia, first aired on NBC in November 1969. Critics worried about negative reaction to "characters made into specific grotesques in animated-cartoon form," which may have seemed like a throwback to "big-eyed and shivering" representations of African Americans on television. But Cosby's race neutrality gave him the ability to massage mainstream boundaries.[85] His playful persona and comedic background assisted the conversion of *Fat Albert and His Friends* into a weekly series on CBS in the 1972–73 season. The *New York Times* concluded that "now there was a childhood crew to link with, laugh at and love."[86]

Humor allowed Cosby to infuse his politics into a television program that served as "not only an entertainment vehicle but also [a program] which conveys a learning experience for children of elementary school age."[87] He fulfilled his dream of becoming a teacher well before he completed his doctorate in education from the University of Massachusetts in 1977. Cosby, a high school *and* college dropout, earned admission into the university's doctoral program based on his life experience. His work on educational television programs, such as *Sesame Street* and *Electric Company*, helped fulfill his practice teaching requirements. Cosby's research reflected his method of merging politics and culture, as he submitted a 267-page dissertation titled "An Integration of the Visual Media via *Fat Albert and the Cosby Kids* into the Elementary School Curriculum as a Teaching Aid and Vehicle to Achieve Increased Learning."[88]

Cosby's educational philosophy rested on the principle that individuals could serve as teachers "in a lot of ways." He posited radio and television as his preferred mediums. "They move the emotions. People learn from the scenes," he said. Cosby had grown to doubt the larger effectiveness of traditional education methods. He remarked that a book was "something you take down from a shelf and place on a coffee table, and nobody reads it. It's not alive," he said. "Film is, and that's what I work in."[89]

Cosby's motion picture debut came in 1971 with the release of *Man and Boy*, a post–Civil War drama centered on the life of a father and his young son in the old West. He personally arranged financing for the $900,000 project after studios communicated that "they didn't like the script and that it couldn't possibly be made for the amount of money [he] said it could."[90] Marvin Miller, the film's producer, noted that particular objections stemmed from the film's perceived "trespassing on the white man's domain by doing a western with black people."[91] But Cosby had climbed high enough in the entertainment industry to resist limitations imposed by white executives unwilling to join him in challenging societal norms. He again demonstrated the level of independence he had achieved in the entertainment industry, which allowed him to develop projects on his own terms. *To All My Friends On Shore*, the gripping story of an odd-job specialist struggling to improve life for his wife and son, followed his debut film in 1972. Cosby conceived and cowrote the film, which raised the issue of race and healthcare through the son's heartbreaking diagnosis with sickle cell anemia. One reviewer noted that "it's so seldom that a television drama comes along with so much to say and says it so well."[92]

Cosby's entrance into motion pictures coincided with a new genre of films that celebrated African American protagonists in violent, criminal roles. Dubbed "blaxploitation" films, their story lines usually revolved around gangster life in urban ghetto settings. Many African American moviegoers applauded the new representations of militant, street-smart heroes, particularly males, although the depiction of underclass lifestyles and behaviors actually worked to reinforce negative racial stereotypes. Cosby's politics of representation registered as opposite of those who produced *Sweet Sweetback's Baadasssss Song, Black Caesar, Super Fly*, and other films within the short-lived blaxploitation genre. "My idea is to raise the quality of the picture a couple of levels so the parents will want to go, with or without the kids," he said.[93] Cosby's requirements for his personal involvement in motion pictures included no cussing or nudity. The strategy had already placed him at the pinnacle of success as a comedian, and it promised more rewards in his new entertainment endeavors.

In the mid-1970s, Cosby starred alongside the nation's leading African American male actor, Sidney Poitier, in three lighthearted action films. *Uptown Saturday Night* followed Harlemites Wardell Franklin (Cosby) and Steve Jackson (Poitier) on their quest to find Jackson's winning lottery ticket, which had been stolen during a heist the night before. In *Let's Do It Again*, Billy Foster (Cosby) and Clyde Williams (Poitier), working-class men from Atlanta, attempted to make a big score while on vacation with their wives in New Orleans. After hypnotizing an underdog prize fighter into believing that he is invincible, the pair set off a firestorm by betting on the fighter and winning big. Poitier and Cosby teamed up once more for a 1977 production titled *A Piece of the Action*. The film centered on two professional criminals, Dave Anderson (Cosby) and Manny Durrell (Poitier), who receive anonymous calls demanding that they donate time and money to a black community center or risk being jailed. The project "was less straight comedy than stew of comedy, action, and romance, seasoned with social justice."[94] All three films projected the politics of representation that both stars espoused. For Cosby, they further cemented his foundation of family entertainment.

In 1972, Cosby said the word "nigger" on public television. He also made disparaging remarks about women and nearly every non-white group in American society. The setting was a television special titled "Bill Cosby on Prejudice," in which he finally made a powerful public statement against racism and other bigoted points of view. Unlike Gregory, who presented his "Light Side, Dark Side" addresses to college students in a highly charged lecture format, Cosby cloaked his daring commentary in a fairly innocuous package. His face appeared almost clownish, with white spectacles painted around his eyes and green coloring applied to his nose. He sat in a chair—typical of his stand-up comedy gigs—wearing casual clothing and smoking a cigar. On a dimly lit set with no backdrops, Cosby delivered a performance within the framework of his politics of representation that allowed him to attack a range of attitudes poisoned by inequality and "otherness." His performance aggressively mocked the type of attitude that his character portrayed. Light background music changed according to his character's targeted shifts in firing off ridiculously bitter and bigoted remarks:

On the elderly: I feel that once you've lost your intelligence or your senses that you should give yourself up. / All they want to do anyway is just sit in the sun on a park bench. I'm not in favor of killing 'em. But there should be some way we could get rid of 'em. / Just get rid of 'em. Nicely, no blood.

On Jewish people: Loan sharks, all of 'em. Jews, no good. / No blood or nothing like that, but just get rid of 'em.

On African Americans: I don't call 'em Black. I call 'em just as I see 'em—*niggers*. / Not one of 'em's got a job. Every one of 'em's on welfare. / You don't have to cause bloodshed or nothing like that because I'm against bloodshed. But just get rid of 'em. Put 'em some place where you can't hear 'em yelling and begging, because they don't have anything. And if you give 'em something, they just dirty it up.

On the Irish: Never seen an Irishman yet that didn't have a big red nose from drinking. / They should get rid of 'em. Get rid of St. Patty's Day, too. Who needs St. Patty? / Just put 'em someplace. Get 'em out of the way. They're a pain in the neck. / Even had a president. Pain in the neck. I didn't vote for him because that's what he was. I saw him for what he was—Irish. And I know he's probably drunk in the White House. Drink too much.

On Italians: In the first place, I don't like the food. / I haven't met an Italian yet [that] wasn't a gangster. / Hate 'em, all of 'em. Every place they go, always talking about their mother, how wonderful she was. Hell, if she's that wonderful, how come you're a criminal? / You should get rid of 'em. All of 'em. Put 'em off some place. No, don't cause no blood. Just gather 'em up.

On Native Americans: This is survival of the fittest, and the Indians weren't fit. / Now, that's it, Indians. Quit begging! Next thing is, they can't handle liquor, so they got no business being here in America. / Need to just put 'em off someplace.

On Southerners: I haven't seen a Southerner that wasn't ignorant yet. / Talk slow, got a drawl. / And they always want to wave a flag, wave a flag, talking about the 'South shall rise again.' / You lost. You'll lose again! Not rise again, you'll lose again. They need to take all them Southerners and just get rid of 'em. Put 'em off someplace because they're embarrassing.

On Midwesterners: People don't know nothing about nothing except going to tent meetings. / You say something about the Bible, they jump right up and want to hurt you. / They should take 'em, put 'em off someplace. I mean, don't shed no blood or nothing like that.

On women: I don't need no woman to have me washing dishes or watching a baby. / If they want to prove something to me, let one of 'em knock me out. They can't do it. / What is it that they want? / Now, they was put here to have babies and wash dishes. / Need to put 'em aside, all them crazy women.

The program closed with Cosby's prejudiced character arguing for the need to "get rid of everybody." After the clown-faced man turns and hears from an off-stage voice that he's a bigot, he states that "it ain't but two of us left, *and I don't care for him.*"[95] The presentation worked well in highlighting the absurdity of prejudice in an entertaining format.

At the time that "Bill Cosby on Prejudice" aired, he stood alone as the African American comedian with the right kind of celebrity capital to deliver a major condemnation of white supremacy across mainstream channels without much backlash. Dick Gregory might have "started the revolution in Negro humor, changing it from an unsophisticated, self-deprecating form of folk art to a polished, outspoken, often needling form of social commentary," but he had also adopted such an intense passion and militancy with respect to civil and human rights agitation that he lost a huge segment of his white following.[96] Cosby's consistent family-oriented messages and programming, on the other hand, positioned him as a highly respectable African American representative of cross-racial communication and progress. He helped relax white Americans' views toward the struggle for African American freedom in the 1960s and beyond. Both Gregory and Cosby made extraordinary strides in helping America laugh and learn, each in his own way. Their pioneering, politicized contributions in the arena of comedy demand their recasting as leading cultural activists in the nation's civil rights era.

Epilogue

Walter Hudson needed help. He weighed about 1,200 pounds, and he lay on his huge belly in the doorway of his bathroom, unable to rise. Rescue workers spent three hours cutting and maneuvering to lift his body. After they finally eased Walter onto wooden planks, it took the strength of eight people to place him back on his bed. His usual two trips per month to the bathroom became even more daunting than before the accident. For psychological and practical reasons, Walter simply could not get out of bed. Gregory arrived and offered assistance in October of 1987. By then, the man once listed by the *Guinness Book of World Records* as the "heaviest man alive" had not stepped outside his home in almost twenty years.[1]

Walter reached out to Gregory through Bob Johnson, editor at *Jet Magazine*. Johnson had run a story that introduced Walter's shocking struggle with obesity to the world.[2] Walter's daily diet reportedly consisted of two boxes of sausages, one pound of bacon, one dozen eggs, a loaf of bread, eight burger and fries combos, three ham steaks, two chickens, four baked potatoes, four sweet potatoes, four heads of broccoli, six quarts of soda, and snacks.[3] Gregory's plan to control Walter's eating habits and reduce his weight to the 200-pound range within three years centered on replacing his food choices with options made available by Dick Gregory Health Enterprises of Chicago. The company marketed a range of health and nutrition products designed to improve people's lives. Walter found encouragement in the thought of becoming one of them. He believed in Gregory, trusted his nutrition recommendations, and soon lost 700 pounds.

Gregory's identity as a health and nutrition guru had grown since the late 1970s. As he participated in marathons and fasts, the international media reported on his strict diet of fruits, vegetables, vitamins, and herbs. A strong endorsement by thirty-six-year-old Muhammad Ali following a triumphant bout with Leon Spinks in 1978 attracted positive attention to Gregory's signature product, Formula Four X. Ali's personal physician said he had "never seen Ali so energetic until after the champ began to take the formula."[4] Endorsements from other professional athletes followed. When Bill "Spaceman" Lee, pitcher for the Boston Red Sox, experienced trauma in his throwing shoulder and lost his place in the club's rotation, Gregory drove to his home with an assortment of nutrients. It helped. "I'd do thirty capsules and pills in one shot," Lee later recalled in his autobiography. "I realize now that it was a form of megavitamin therapy, and that Dick was way ahead of his time."[5] Willie Stargell requested that Gregory supply nutrients for him and other Pittsburgh Pirates players in 1979. The team won the World Series that year. Stargell, the thirty-eight-year-old first baseman whom Gregory had placed on a regiment of seventy-six vitamin pills per day, earned the honor of MVP.[6]

By design, athletes and other celebrities enjoyed early access to Gregory's health products. "The reason I wanted athletes to use my formula [first] was to take away the stigma of it being a food 'for poverty-stricken people,'" Gregory recalled. "The celebrity athletes definitely helped with the publicity for Formula Four X, but I mainly wanted them to take away its negative image before it was introduced to the world."[7] The larger goal of Gregory's health and nutrition endeavor involved ending world hunger. Like Martin Luther King Jr., Gregory's civil rights activism led him toward a broader human rights agenda. He believed that Formula Four X provided a safe, affordable food alternative that could sustain poor and starving people everywhere.

In 1984, Gregory fasted for 167 days to draw attention to famine in Ethiopia. Average protein consumption in the country fell 20 percent below the minimum, which caused "chronic undernourishment."[8] Gregory's outrage over projections of one million deaths in 1985 included a racial component: "If it was in any white country no one would [have to] tell us that."[9] He made ten trips to East Africa in 1985, during which his nutrition formula met testing and won approval by the Ethiopian government. After twenty-four malnourished children showed "marked improvement" following two weeks of treatment with Formula Four X, the self-taught nutritionist's company fulfilled an order for 100 cases of formula and 100 cases of food bars.[10]

Gregory's lucrative new venture also included a program for weight loss. Walter Hudson knew about Formula Four X and Gregory's $100 million contract with Cernitin America to sell (by mail order and independent distributorship) Dick Gregory's Slim-Safe Bahamian Diet.[11] It was marketed as an "all-natural powder concentrate that can be mixed with fruit juices to form a great tasting drink."[12] Before Gregory's introduction to Walter, the former comedian had begun assisting several morbidly obese people with losing weight. He personally funded their transition to his new but short-lived international health institute in Nassau, Bahamas. Ronald High, Gregory's first patient, embraced the gift. He checked in at 801 pounds and lost 243 pounds within five months.[13] But Walter's psychological block prevented him from following Ronald. Gregory staged a press conference during which he challenged Walter to courageously step outside his home. It doubled as an ultimatum. "He told us he just can't do it," Gregory announced with sadness.[14] He and Walter said goodbye that day, and Walter said goodbye to the world five years later, having gained back the 700 pounds that Gregory helped him lose. Reports indicated that his body remained in his home on the night of his death "because it wouldn't fit through the front door."[15]

Gregory recalled one of his funniest stories associated with the sale of Slim Safe, which raked in approximately $15 million in its first year. At the Black Caucus Convention Expo in Washington, a 300-pound woman visited Gregory's booth to discuss the $22 cost for two cans of the product (one sixteen-ounce can regularly sold for $19.95):

> "Dick Gregory," she said. "Look at me. I'm a welfare sister, a Black person just like you. I weigh over three hundred pounds. How do you expect me to pay twenty-two dollars to buy that stuff?"
>
> I looked at this big woman. "If you go to the supermarket and pay enough money to get as big as you are, why should I get it off of you for free? You are out of your mind."
>
> She said, "Let me get two cans, my man!" She laughed so hard that they had to pick her up off the floor. People just started lining up behind her to buy the product.[16]

Gregory's success ripened the opportunity for his second mail-order business, Correction Connection, Inc. The enterprise offered assistance to individuals seeking to break addictions to drugs, alcohol, and cigarettes. It was another golden idea, although it would soon fail along with Gregory's other businesses because of his characteristic nonconformity and capriciousness. Gregory overstretched his resources by pledging $1 million to at least twelve organizations serving underprivileged groups. His allocation of 10 percent of all earnings toward an "offensive" designed to promote health education among youth—employing Veronica Ali, wife of Muhammad Ali, as one of his millionaire employees at a salary of $6 million—ran counter to the best interest of the company.[17] His purchase of a failing beachfront hotel in Florida for $7.5 million and acquisition of more properties in the South and Midwest indicated the absence of effective management and planning. Yet Gregory charged forward with his aims to erect centers designed to "create a glamorous aura around health care and nutrition" and, ultimately, "creat[e] more Black billionaires than any person or entity in the history of this country" through distributorships and other inclusive opportunities.[18] The dreams would not materialize. In 1988, Gregory began a draining series of court proceedings against his business partner and secretary, alleging that they withheld royalties and conned him out of his 80-percent stake in Correction Connection. "Because of the movement and Dr. King, I never let myself get bitter or angry," he wrote. "I never lost sight of my work for the people and the Movement as the court battle lingered."[19] It ended three years later with Gregory's money, company, and family farm in Massachusetts having vanished.

The tumble had become too familiar for a once-great public figure with seemingly too much experience in entertainment and business to lose it all *again*. But the failed outcome once more demonstrated Gregory's unwavering commitment to the values and strategies he developed while participating in the movement, even if they ran counter to his best interests. The promise of widespread economic empowerment made possible by his businesses connected well with the idea of African American uplift. For Gregory, it mattered far less if an alternate route may have better protected his financial status. Paying exorbitant salaries to Veronica Ali and others served as Gregory's method of funding comrades in the movement. He had done the same at the height of his earning power as a comedian, although he seemingly learned no lesson in waging such an individual war against white supremacy. Gregory also seemed blind to the cost of providing intense medical care for dozens of obese and malnourished people. Indeed, he rejected capitalism and championed humanity in a manner that again left him and his family broke. Gregory's waywardness damaged his unique role as an activist. Only a few other African American celebrities could have matched his ability to tap resources from the grassroots level to the Hollywood A-list, and neither of them followed his kamikaze style.

Gregory's amazing rise and fall in the 1980s escaped well over half of Generation X, the millions of latchkey kids born from the late 1960s through the early 1980s.[20] His exceptional success in the business world received fair coverage in the media, particularly by African American reporters, but it by no means matched the attention commanded by celebrity entertainers. Generation Xers have little grasp of Gregory's civil and human rights record. Millennials do not recognize his name at all. By the end of the 1980s, a noticeable loss of social and political capital among young Americans proved to be the cost of Gregory's late-1960s militancy. He never recaptured the nation's ear as effectively as he did when he used comedy as a form of social mediation.

Gregory spent the 1990s fumbling his limited opportunities to regain a place in the nation's conscience. He launched his "Capital Clean Sweep" program in Washington, DC, to help reduce the city's alarming homicide rate. While noble, Gregory's plan featured a radicalism that diluted its merit—he called for community members to join him in confronting alleged drug dealers with the ultimatum to "leave or kill us all."[21] His assertion that the Centers for Disease Control and Prevention abducted twenty-seven African American children over a two-year period for medical research (the "Atlanta Child Murders") ruffled feathers.[22] Gregory further charged the US government with complicity in the crack cocaine epidemic that plagued many African American communities in the 1980s and 1990s.[23] Mainstream media listened but paid little attention to Gregory's developing tendency to promote conspiracy theories.

In March 1992, someone stole a can of bee pollen tablets worth ten dollars from a store in St. Louis. The clerk called the police. Approximately fifteen minutes later, an officer spotted Gregory nearby. He had recently arrived in his native St. Louis to support Katherine Dunham's fast against US policy toward Haiti. The sixty-year-old Gregory fit the description, but he exploded because of his perceived harassment as a suspect. Despite soon being told that he was "free to go," Gregory cursed the officer, which led to his apprehension for suspicion of disturbing the peace. The dilemma continued. Gregory insisted on formal arrest after transport to two police stations. He recalled the sentiment expressed by one African American clerk to the apprehending officer: "Oh, you have fucked up now!"[24] The potential headline of a public figure's false arrest carried the elements of a national news story, but Gregory's characteristic odd behavior pushed the incident well past the margin of important news.

In 1995, the unpredictable Gregory attempted a comeback after more than twenty years away from comedy. His stand-up act failed to generate enough buzz to return him to the A-list. Those familiar with Gregory as a comedian in the 1960s may have been disappointed with the "grizzly-bearded, lean and determinedly warm fellow who, as Mr. Gregory puts it, looks more like 'Uncle Remus' than Uncle Remus." He simply could not re-create the fiery satirical routines that once catapulted him to mainstream success. From the 1970s through the 1990s, America's gains in race relations opened doors for new comedians to blossom as crossover acts. Because of the wide visibility of Pryor, Murphy, Robin Harris, Martin Lawrence, Paul Mooney, Wanda Sykes, D. L. Hughley, Chris Rock, and other edgy comic stars in mainstream entertainment, Gregory's return as a comedian carried very little punch or novelty. Ben Brantley of the *New York Times* recorded that "the performer once perceived as black America's answer to Mort Sahl now seems far closer to Will Rogers." Brantley assessed the humor that Gregory described as "conscious comedy" as giving off "the comforting feeling of the talkative, mildly eccentric relative who arrives at every big family gathering with an arsenal of fiercely held convictions and off-center bits of advice."[25]

In *Callus On My Soul*, Gregory's autobiography published in 2000, he challenged readers to "name one other movement in the history of this planet in which *every single leader* has been murdered."[26] The riddle fed into his belief that powerful white Americans have silenced, destroyed, and eliminated serious threats to the establishment. According to Gregory, not only were these powerful whites responsible for the murders of civil rights leaders, such as Medgar Evers, Martin Luther King Jr., and Malcolm X, but they also carried involvement in the deaths of Abraham Lincoln, John F. Kennedy, Lenny Bruce, John Lennon, Ron Brown, Betty Shabazz, Ennis Cosby, and others. Gregory continued to promote his belief in dozens of conspiracy theories, and his rants often referenced his FBI file (released in 1977 following a Freedom of Information Act request). The documents revealed J. Edgar Hoover's 1968 directive that the Chicago office "neutralize" the satirical humorist. Hoover even suggested the use of La Cosa Nostra, a mafia organization, as a possible tool in the initiative. Considering the psychological impact of this and other serious threats against Gregory's life, his larger participation in the fight to end segregation and discrimination, and the roller coaster highs and lows that come with entertainment stardom, it is perhaps understandable that Gregory may have thought and acted in ways incomprehensible to many.

Hollywood finally honored Gregory with a Walk of Fame Star in 2015, more than half a century after he made history as the nation's first African American stand-up comedian to cross over. "You know damn good and well why it took so long," Gregory quipped. "I've been a bad boy."[27] It is entirely reasonable that Gregory could have become just as accomplished in the television and film industry as his counterpart Cosby, but his passionate involvement in the African American struggle for freedom simply led him to make choices that separated him from the spoils of fame. "He gave it up for *us*," Cosby explained during a guest appearance on *Arsenio* in 2014.[28] For those who may forever question why he operated with such a maverick spirit and ran with unusual decisions despite the high costs, Gregory's autobiography offers a succinct explanation: "Perhaps racism made me this way."[29]

"Baba" Dick Gregory passed away on August 19, 2017. He had been admitted to Sibley Memorial Hospital in Washington, DC, a week prior. What began as a urinary tract infection "wrecked havoc on my father's slim frame," Christian Gregory shared.[30] Hundreds gathered for Gregory's celebration of life and homegoing service at City of Praise Family Ministries in Landover, Maryland, including Bill Cosby, Minister Louis Farrakhan, Maxine Waters, Myrlie Evers-Williams, and Stevie Wonder (who credited Gregory with recommending a personalized diet plan in 1999 that saved his life). One segment featured the children of African American political and cultural heroes. Reena Evers-Everette, Martin Luther King III, Rain Pryor, and Ilyasah Shabazz (daughter of Malcolm X) roused the audience with their group appearance. So too did Gregory's daughter Ayanna, who performed an original song titled "Daughter of the Movement." That she maintained her composure through such a powerful and emotionally gripping performance was awe inspiring.

The seven-hour ceremony honoring the life of an American legend received little media coverage. No network televised even a portion of the service. TV One, a cable network centered on African American viewership, provided online coverage via live stream. Announcement of Gregory's death had been widely communicated by the news media, but his legacy did not register as significant enough for any large network to dispatch its crews. The snub demonstrated the nation's continued lack of awareness and appreciation of Gregory's contributions to the advancement of democracy and equality. The *Emmy Awards*, a nationally televised awards program produced by the Television Academy, aired nearly a month after Gregory's passing but failed to include him in its "In Memoriam" segment.

Speaking on behalf of the Gregory family, Christian Gregory called the omission "highly disrespectful."[31] One of Cosby's tweets about Gregory after his death struck a similar chord: "In Memory of Dick Gregory 'An Unacknowledged Hero.' "[32] Gregory rose from extreme poverty in St. Louis to become the Jackie Robinson of stand-up comedy and a champion of civil and human rights issues. His story must be included in civil rights and American historical narratives alongside other icons who courageously and tirelessly struggled to push the country closer to its founding principles.

Cosby rose to the pinnacle of his career in the 1980s, cheered on by fans of every generation. He survived a mediocre end to the 1970s as the mainstream appetite welcomed more daring comedic voices. Richard Pryor's uncensored language and discussion of street life astonished America's increasingly integrated audiences, and newcomer Eddie Murphy's dynamism and explosive talent quickly turned him into a star.[33] It seemed as if Cosby could not compete. "Some people are disappointed because I still do a family show," Cosby said, but he felt content as long as his comedy served as "something [that] pulls and holds a family together, and makes them laugh at themselves."[34] His television project that debuted in 1984, *The Cosby Show*, may have been a reward from the comedy gods. The program centered on a successful African American couple—Cosby as Cliff Huxtable, a doctor, and Phylicia Rashad as Claire Huxtable, a lawyer—and their humorous but meaningful journey forward while rearing five children. The atypical representation proved rewarding. Cosby's vision resulted in "the most profitable show in the history of television."[35]

Critics of *The Cosby Show* initially attacked Cosby's portrayal of African American life in the Reagan era. Ronald Smith noted the barrage of derisive questions that Cosby fielded from the press:

> Aren't you out of touch? How many whites will be on the show? Will you show the real black American family? What about social problems? What about white versus black? Isn't it a fairy tale to portray blacks as doctors and lawyers? How come you don't talk like George Jefferson or Fred Sanford—isn't that real black dialect? And why aren't you having the family live in the ghetto?[36]

Darryl Pinckney of the *New York Times* concluded that Cosby's brilliance had been missed by his early critics, which included African Americans. Pinckney reminded all that "emphasis was not on what [the Huxtables] were but rather on who they were, on the morality of their choices and what they were doing with their advantages." Despite Cosby's slight decline in the late 1970s and early 1980s, his long-standing presence as a "comic persona that was universal while remaining black" promised an audience.[37] Yet even the networks hesitated to buy in after hearing Cosby's initial pitch. ABC eventually "backed off," and NBC sought to test the sitcom's viability by offering a contract for only six episodes. Cosby insisted on starting with a thirteen-episode agreement, and he eventually won.[38]

The Cosby Show entertained audiences for eight seasons. Its humor, positivity, and family-oriented themes appealed to every major demographic. Millions of American families found Cosby and his television show relatable, prompting Pinckney to regard the comic star as "the black face that's a mirror for everyone."[39] As Cliff Huxtable, Cosby communicated with America through his relationships with the show's main characters. Through Sondra, the oldest child, who graduated from Princeton and married a handsome doctor, he displayed the gentle pride and satisfaction that most parents hope to experience following truly successful child rearing. Through Denise, the quirky and rebellious second child, he exhibited a hilarious blend of frustration and bewilderment in attempting to understand his teenage daughter. (The younger demographic responded so well to Cliff and Denise that Cosby developed a spinoff, *A Different World*, which followed Denise in her college years away from home.) The most powerful relationship that Cosby developed on the show may have centered on the psychological tugs-of-war between Cliff and his only son, Theo, as he nurtured him from boyhood to manhood. Real-life Cosby's only biological son, Ennis, provided the inspiration for the character. The genuine closeness between Cliff and Theo certainly highlighted *The Cosby Show*, and it reflected Cosby's method of educating through entertainment.

Like Ennis Cosby, Theo Huxtable demonstrated a learning disability that forced his dad to exercise patience along with tough love. One of the show's most memorable scenes featured Cliff finding a school assignment on which Theo had earned a D and then teaching Theo a stern lesson about excelling in life rather than settling for mediocrity. Young Theo responded with a touching emotional outburst regarding his perceived inability to match Cliff's professional achievements:

> You're a doctor and Mom's a lawyer. And you're both successful and everything, and that's great. But maybe, I was born to be a regular person, and have a regular life. If you weren't a

doctor, I wouldn't love *you* less. Because you're my dad. And so, instead of acting disappointed, because I'm not like you, maybe you can just accept who I am, and love me anyway. Because I'm your son.

The audience responded with prolonged applause. Cosby, as Cliff, held a solemn stare for a few seconds to further dramatize the moment. But, ever the gifted comedian, he soon quelled the emotional tension with an outburst of his own that rocked the audience into thunderous laughter:

Theo, that's the *dumbest* thing I've ever heard in my life. No wonder you get Ds in everything! Now, you are afraid to try because you're afraid that your brain is going to explode, and it's going to ooze out of your ears. Now I'm telling you, you are going to try as hard as you can. And you're gonna do it because *I said so*. I am your father. I brought you in this world, and I'll take you out.[40]

While the endless situational humor explored through the Huxtable children, including young Vanessa and toddler Rudy, helped drive viewership, the loving partnership between Cliff and Claire proved equally compelling. The power couple maintained a darling relationship that occasionally pitted the two of them against the children and even one another. A lesson stood to be learned in each contest, one that often left viewers happy, optimistic, and eager for the next episode. Indeed, some even saw *The Cosby Show* as more than just a weekly television escape. The lifestyle and vibe of the show actually carried hope for millions of Americans. Children envisioned Cliff as *their* dad, Claire as *their* mom. Particularly among African American young adults, *The Cosby Show* represented the type of professional and personal happiness that was possible if society were equal and fair. Cosby's family comedy repositioned him as a comedy giant, ballooned his net worth to more than $300 million, and cemented him in the annals of history as "America's favorite dad."

Another great achievement of *The Cosby Show* may have been that it finally granted one of the most gifted comedians of the twentieth century the latitude to take on certain social issues. Since removing race from his act and public persona in the early 1960s, Cosby calculated his moves in the entertainment world with precision. He had previously worked to advance the struggle for African American freedom only in spots while attempting to avoid public association with controversial race issues. But Cosby demonstrated willingness, or perhaps acknowledgement of his license to speak out with little chance of career jeopardy, following the astounding success of *The Cosby Show*. He promoted HBCUs on the show by sporting college and university gear during episodes. The gesture thrilled and inspired African American youth. Some watched to see if Cosby would wear their school's gear, and some became aware of schools to which they could apply. Ta-Nehisi Coates suggested that Cosby "elevated himself from black middle-class ambassador to bona fide Race Man" with his 1988 donation of $20 million to Spelman College.[41] His perceivably heightened identification with racial uplift and public giving elevated his status as a role model among many in African American communities in the 1980s.

In the 1990s, Cosby operated with a new politics centered on public commentary and open calls for advancement in African American life and culture. On representations of African Americans on television, Cosby expressed doubt that "anybody's learned a damn thing from watching [*The Cosby Show*] for eight years."[42] He strongly admonished writers and producers responsible for perpetuating African American stereotypes in his Television Academy Hall of Fame induction speech:

> These shows have black women with their hands on their hips with none of these images graduating from college or making a better world. Colored, black, Negro, African American, God knows who I'll be in 10 years from now. However, we are not those negatories [sic] that you see. These are drive-by images. Television has been wonderful to me, but in 1992, I'm asking people to stop this horrible massacre of images that are being shown on the screen now.[43]

It previewed a theme that would pour from Cosby in subsequent pointed outbursts. In 1992, *TV Guide* documented Cosby's striking disapproval of African American sitcoms that popularized what he deemed as nothing more than updated versions of characters such as "JJ" from *Good Times*, the 1970s sitcom centered on an African American family in Chicago living well below the poverty line: "It isn't fair. It isn't us. I want us to graduate."[44]

Cosby continued to demonstrate the seriousness of his calls for better-quality television programming when he attempted to buy NBC, the network that he had made number one. It would have been a remarkable story, especially given that Cosby got his big break on the network's *I Spy* program nearly thirty years prior. Despite a response from the network's parent company that "NBC is not for sale," the attempted purchase served as representative of Cosby's new outspokenness and activism.[45]

Cosby's new politics in the 1990s also included direct action, which broke from his long pattern of contributing money to crises rather than leadership. When African American homicide offending and victimization rates surged in the early 1990s, particularly among males in the eighteen- to twenty-four age range, Cosby joined the front lines of the antiviolence movement.[46] At Thomas Jefferson High School in Brooklyn, a campus aggrieved by nearly fifty deaths among its student population dating back to the late 1980s, Cosby showed up days after a double homicide rattled the community. Fifteen-year-old Khalil Sumpter shot and killed sixteen-year-old Tyrone Sinkler and seventeen-year-old Ian Moore at point-blank range in a school hallway. A friend of both deceased boys was found dead in his home hours later with a gunshot wound to the head.[47] Cosby stood shoulder to shoulder with Principal Carol Burt Beck and dozens more in protest against the violence. He spoke of a lesson he learned from a voice in a Philadelphia church: "Lord, there's a stranger in the house. How the stranger got in nobody knows. But you've got to rid your house of the stranger because the stranger does no good."[48] His comments certainly did not match the oratory of King or Jackson, but Cosby's mere presence signaled an important shift in his approach to associating himself with racial issues.

In 1994, the *New York Amsterdam* described Cosby as an "outspoken critic of Black-on-Black crime." The characterization followed a Cosby address in Bermuda during which he challenged residents of the island to clean up its ghettoes. "Why are there only drug dealers in certain neighborhoods?" he asked. "They're there because you're letting it happen and you're satisfied to let it happen."[49] No one could have predicted the terrible irony that befell Cosby just a few years later. On January 16, 1997, a Ukrainian immigrant shot and killed his twenty-seven-year-old son, Ennis, in a "middle to upper-middle-income, predominately white community" in Los Angeles.[50] The two intersected after Ennis pulled over to change a flat tire, and the assailant—en route to rob a drug connection—spotted his Mercedes and elected to make a quick score. Cosby received the tragic news while on the set of his late-1990s sitcom, *Cosby*.

American media and the public grieved with their beloved icon. "The initial shock over Ennis Cosby's shooting turned into an outpouring of support for Bill," Smith wrote. "News reporters didn't hide their sadness, acknowledging that Bill was such a beloved figure that most everyone felt he was a 'member of the family.' "⁵¹ Many Americans likely recall the news broadcasts covered by scores of reporters at Cosby's New York home that day. The four-word statement Cosby gave on Ennis's death touched millions: "He was my hero." But fewer may remember the sentiment he shared less than two weeks later upon orchestrating a two-hour interview with CBS anchor Dan Rather: "I think it's time for me to tell the people that we have to laugh," Cosby said. "We've got to laugh."⁵²

Cosby's navigation of the entertainment world in the 1960s and beyond produced a cultural and social relevance that made Americans care not only about his work, but also about his life. Unlike Gregory, Cosby experienced no difficulty being celebrated and understood by the majority of Americans in the decades following his rise to fame. Hollywood rewarded his contributions to entertainment with a Walk of Fame Star in 1977, and President George W. Bush bestowed the Medal of Freedom on the legendary comedian in 2002. Scores of other awards fell in between. Most considered "America's favorite dad" incapable of any serious missteps that could threaten his popularity, but his speech at a 2004 NAACP event commemorating the fiftieth anniversary of *Brown v. Board* set off a controversy that lasted months. Cosby's remarks became labeled as the "Pound Cake Speech" because of his angst over African American males dying over matters as trivial as a piece of pound cake. He offended millions with his candid thoughts regarding the depressed state of low-income African American communities:

> Ladies and gentlemen, in our cities and public schools we have fifty percent drop out. In our own neighborhood, we have men in prison. No longer is a person embarrassed because they're pregnant without a husband. No longer is a boy considered an embarrassment if he tries to run away from being the father of the unmarried child.
>
> Looking at the incarcerated, these are not political criminals. These are people going around stealing Coca Cola. People getting shot in the back of the head over a piece of pound cake! Then we all run out and are outraged, "The cops shouldn't have shot him." What the hell was he doing with the pound cake in his hand?
>
> Just forget telling your child to go to the Peace Corps. It's right around the corner. It's standing on the corner. It can't speak English. It doesn't want to speak English. I can't even

talk the way these people talk. "Why you ain't where you is go, ra." I don't know who these people are. And I blamed the kid until I heard the mother talk.

Basketball players, multimillionaires can't write a paragraph. Football players, multimillionaires, can't read. Yes. Multimillionaires. Well, *Brown v. Board of Education*, where are we today? It's there. They paved the way. What did we do with it[?] The white man, he's laughing, got to be laughing. Fifty percent drop out, rest of them in prison.

We are not Africans. Those people are not Africans; they don't know a damned thing about Africa. With names like Shaniqua, Shaligua, Mohammed, and all that crap, and all of them are in jail.[53]

Following the event, Cosby faced a groundswell of criticism for the first time in his career. He refused to back down. "I'm going to keep on saying what I've been saying," he declared in a speech to the National Association for Equal Opportunity in Higher Education.[54] Scholar Michael Eric Dyson led the rebuttal. "Cosby never acknowledges that most poor blacks don't have a choice about these things," he said.[55] Ta-Nehisi Coates slammed Cosby for popularizing a narrative of African American culture as "bastardized and pathological."[56] More critics charged Cosby with being elitist and out of touch with issues affecting African Americans living near or below subsistence level. Television personality Judge Greg Mathis supported Cosby by asserting his "right to provide a fatherly role of critiquing and administering tough love."[57] Columnist Leonard Pitts Jr. suggested that Cosby's only "mistake" lay in speaking publicly. Pitts applauded the comedian's openness in discussing racial issues and humorously concluded that if someone had spiked Cosby's Jell-O, then all of America needed to have the same dessert.[58]

Humor is the glaring omission from Cosby's delivery of his "Pound Cake Speech." The gifted storyteller who achieved fame and fortune by using anecdotes to break down racial barriers failed to employ the same delicate approach in his message to and about African Americans. Keegan-Michael Key and Jordan Peele, stars of the Comedy Central television program *Key & Peele*, perhaps took note prior to the development of their "East/West College Bowl" sketch (which, to date, has garnered more than 50 million views on YouTube). They, too, launched an attack on the creative license that some African American parents have taken in naming their children, but they laced it with comedy. After two white male commentators opened a parody of a pregame introduction of college football players, Key and Peele alternated portraying the players and voicing their names and institutions. Included among the intentionally ridiculing names are "D'Squarius Green Jr.," "L'Carpetron Dookmarriott," "Shakiraquan T.G.I.F. Carter," and "Scoish Velociraptor Maloish." Nearly all of the players were to be perceived as African American or biracial until the very last introduction when a white football player (not portrayed by Key or Peele) introduced himself as "Dan Smith." Yet no backlash sprung because the masses accepted the delivery under the umbrella of comedy.[59]

"Substitute Teacher," *Key & Peele's* even more popular sketch based on the perceived unorthodoxy of African American naming culture, has amassed more than 150 million views on YouTube. The dilemma of a teacher antagonized by the "normal" names of white suburban students after spending twenty years teaching kids in the "inner city" again proved easily digestible by many African Americans and the nation at large because of its comical delivery. During his very first roll call, the teacher experienced pushback after pronouncing Jaqueline as "jay-QWELL-in," Blake as "buh-LAH-kay," and Aaron as "a-A-ron." The punch line featured a lone African American student, "Timothy," who immediately accepted the pronunciation of his name as "tuh-MOE-thee" by saying "PREE-zent" in response. The humor worked in masking an otherwise offensive and controversial commentary on African American naming culture. Cosby's mid-2000s addresses on the state of black America, conversely, carried little to no humor. The ramifications of his frankness would reach farther than he could have possibly imagined in years to come.[60]

Regardless of his failed delivery, Cosby's mid-2000s remarks reflected his long emphasis on education and middle-class values as tools of racial uplift. Consistency in purpose rank among his greatest attributes. The "pound cake" dilemma resulted in the publication of *Come On, People!: On the Path from Victims to Victors*, a collaborative effort between Cosby and Harvard psychiatrist Alvin Poussaint designed as an empowerment guide. It centered on parenting, education, and personal responsibility, highlighted by several "call-outs"—uplifting words of wisdom from those who had overcome struggle. Cosby and Poussaint donated 5,000 copies to schools and prisons nationwide in an effort to reach locations "where young people have had difficulty."[61]

Cosby survived the public relations crisis surrounding his comments on African American life and culture. But beginning in late 2014, a firestorm of reports about his sexual proclivities irreparably tarnished his image. They culminated in his conviction on three counts of aggravated indecent assault in June of 2018. A jury found him guilty of drugging and sexually violating Andrea Constand, a thirty-two-year-old woman at the time, whom he met in her role as director of operations for the Temple women's basketball program. The assault took place at Cosby's Philadelphia residence in 2004.

Constand and Cosby settled a civil suit in 2005. Following Constand's lead, dozens more women came forward to share their stories of victimization by Cosby. Their accounts spanned a fifty-year period and included harrowingly similar details, but all except Constand's exceeded the statute of limitations for filing criminal charges. Constand's criminal case against Cosby, in this context, registered a meaningful victory for Cosby's other victims and thousands of sexual assault survivors who closely followed his trial. Most applauded the three- to ten-year prison sentence he began serving in September 2018.

Jurors reported that the deposition given by Cosby in response to Constand's 2005 civil suit proved to be the most damning piece of evidence in the criminal case. Although the deposition had been sealed, a federal judge ordered it unsealed in the interest of the public good because of Cosby's possible hypocrisy as a "public moralist."[62] The irony of Cosby's mid-2000s addresses on the state of black America being a determining factor in his criminal trial is astounding.

Cosby's incredible downturn begs the question of how to reconcile his brilliant professional career and the nefarious behavior in his personal life. For some, there can be no reconciliation. BET, Bounce TV, and TV Land responded to the millions of Americans who swiftly and decisively condemned the comedy giant by taking reruns of *The Cosby Show* off the air. Many institutions of higher education, including Boston College, Notre Dame, Temple, and Yale, revoked Cosby's honorary degrees. The Constand case finally exposed to mainstream America the depth of the dual persona that Cosby constructed in the 1960s. He had guarded his impoverished upbringing, exposure to domestic violence, dropouts from high school and college, and other sensitive information about his personal life so well that the nation grappled with accepting reports of its "favorite dad's" criminal behavior. Until Constand's case, Dr. Cosby had cornered his space in the nation's conscience as *the* cross-cultural, middle-class-American-male values representative.

TV One continued to air episodes of *The Cosby Show* after other stations pulled the plug following Cosby's conviction. The network and

Cosby's remaining fans would likely advocate for the separation of his professional achievements from his private life, similar to the nuanced treatment provided to other cultural celebrities with genius talent along with guilt of criminal and/or morally reprehensible acts against women (e.g., Woody Allen, Mel Gibson, Tupac Shakur, Mike Tyson). While the public abhors their alleged transgressions, it also tolerates continued discussion and consumption of their works. The longevity and multiplicity of Cosby's additional alleged crimes cannot be ignored, but, for more than a few, neither can his engineering of a plan that effected measurable gains for African Americans in entertainment and larger society.

Eighty-two-year-old Cosby, the "Jackie Robinson of television," indeed executed strategic jumps over Jim Crow during an era that some historians identify as the Second American Revolution. The paradox of his rise and fall is certain to command the attention of media, scholars, the public, and courts for the foreseeable future.

During the Civil Rights Movement, Gregory and Cosby asserted themselves as champions of the struggle in the comic arena. Their stand-up acts in the 1960s and early 1970s hinged on a politics of representation that communicated African Americans' frustrations and hopes. The nation responded favorably to the rise of both comedic talents, although it quickly discarded one and celebrated the other. While Gregory demonstrated how radical individualism could create an irreversible barrier between performer and society, Cosby established near-complete dissociation from controversial race issues, at least publicly, as an alternate method to defeat Jim Crow. His careful navigation of the entertainment world in the 1960s and beyond produced a cultural and social relevance that made Americans care about not only his work, but also his life. The legacies of Gregory and Cosby at the height of the Civil Rights Movement parallel the historic racial uplift debates between the ideologies of Delaney and Douglass, Washington and Du Bois, and Malcolm X and Dr. King. Gregory and Cosby were indeed activists who occupied unique and opposing positions within the movement, and they helped usher in advancement for African Americans and larger American society using creative voices of protest against racism.

Notes

Introduction

1. Dexter B. Gordon, "Humor in African American Discourse: Speaking of Oppression," *Journal of Black Studies* 29, no. 2 (November 1998): 274.

2. Lawrence Mintz, "Standup Comedy as Social and Cultural Mediation," *American Quarterly* 37, no. 1 (Spring 1985): 71.

3. *The Late Show with Stephen Colbert*, "Dave Chappelle Spoke Up At A Town Hall In Ohio," *YouTube*. Online Video Clip, August 3, 2017, https://www.youtube.com/watch?v=ZLTNwPoX1Qo.

4. Bill Cosby, interview by the author, telephone, December 10, 2013.

5. Aram Goudsouzian, *Sidney Poitier: Man, Actor, Icon* (Chapel Hill, NC: University of North Carolina Press, 2003), 112; Suzanne Smith, *Dancing in the Streets: Motown and the Politics of Detroit* (New York, NY: Holt Paperbacks, 2007); Jules Tygiel, *Baseball's Great Experiment: Jackie Robinson and His Legacy* (New York, NY: Oxford University Press, 2008).

6. See Bambi Haggins, *Laughing Mad: The Black Comic Persona in Post-Soul America* (New Brunswick, NJ: Rutgers University Press, 2007); Patrick Miller and David Wiggins, eds., *Sport and the Color Line: Black Athletes and Race Relations in Twentieth Century America* (New York, NY: Routledge, 2003); Emily Raymond, *Stars for Freedom: Hollywood, Black Celebrities, and the Civil Rights Movement* (Seattle, WA: University of Washington Press, 2015); Brian Ward, *Just My Soul Responding: Rhythm and Blues, Black Consciousness and Race Relations* (Oakland, CA: University of California Press, 1998); David Wiggins, *Glory Bound: Black Athletes in a White America* (Syracuse, NY: Syracuse University Press, 1997).

7. Larry Glen, "Bill Cosby: The Clown as Straight Man," *Tuesday Magazine*, October 1965, 28.

8. "Master Mimic Bill Cosby: An Electronic Mark Twain," *Life Magazine*, March 15, 1968, 40.

9. Peter Coutros, "Here He Is, Folks, Dick Gregory: Fizz, Crackle, Zap, Ba-Room," *Daily News*, June 22, 1970, 42.

10. Alfred Aronowitz, "Gregory, Brain Surgeon," *New York Post*, June 10, 1970, 16.

11. A. S. Doc Young, "'Bill Cosby Is Not Malcolm X, He's Bill Cosby,'" *New York Times*, December 21, 1969.

Chapter 1

1. Dick Gregory, *Nigger: An Autobiography* by Dick Gregory (New York: Pocket Books, 1964), 41.

2. Dick Gregory, *Callus on My Soul: A Memoir* (New York: Kensington Publishing Corp., 2000), 10.

3. Bill Cosby, *Childhood* (New York, NY: G. P. Putnam's Sons, 1991), 52–53, 117.

4. James Neal Primm, *Lion of the Valley: St. Louis, Missouri, 1764–1980* (St. Louis, MO: Missouri Historical Society Press, 1981), 396, 398.

5. Robert Asher, "Documents of the Race Riot at East Saint Louis," *Journal of the Illinois State Historical Society* 65, no. 3 (Autumn 1972): 327.

6. Primm, 413–14.

7. US Census Bureau. *Volume 2: Population: Reports by States Alabama-Montana, 1164 pp., 1915 ed.*, http://www2.census.gov/prod2/decennial/documents/36894832v2.zip.; US Census Bureau. *Fourteenth Census of the United States. State Compendium . . . Statistics of population occupations, agriculture, manufactures, and mines and quarries . . . 1926-1926. 49 pamphlets, Massachusetts to Montana*, http://www2.census.gov/prod2/decennial/documents/06229686v20-25.zip.

8. US Census Bureau. *Vol. 3, Part 1. Population: Reports by States Alabama-Missouri, 1389 pp., 1932 ed.*, http://www2.census.gov/prod2/decennial/documents/10612963v3p1.zip.

9. *Nigger*, 26.

10. Primm, 441.

11. *Nigger*, 25.

12. *Nigger*, 9.

13. Dick Gregory, *Dick Gregory Talks Turkey* (Narbeth, PA: Rhino Entertainment, 2000; originally released in 1962).

14. Ronald L. Smith, *Cosby: The Life of a Comic Legend* (Amherst, NY: Prometheus Books, 1997), 8.

15. Russell F. Weigley, ed., *Philadelphia: A 300-Year History* (New York: W.W. Norton & Co, Inc., 1982), 615–16.

16. Bill Cosby, *Wonderfulness* (Burbank, CA: Warner Bros. Records, Inc., 1966).

17. Smith, 9.

18. Gregory, *Callus on My Soul*, 14–20.

19. Smith, 16.

20. "'Raceless' Bill Cosby," *Ebony*, May 1, 1964, 132.

21. U.S. Census Bureau. *Volume 3: Population: Reports by States Nebraska-Wyoming, 1228 pp., 1913 ed.*, http://www2.census.gov/prod2/decennial/documents/36894832v3.zip.; U.S. Census Bureau. *Vol. 3, Part 2. Population: Reports by States Montana-Wyoming, 1395 pp., 1932 ed.*, http://www2.census.gov/prod2/decennial/documents/10612982v3p2.zip.

22. Weigley, 588.

23. Smith, 7, 10, 12.

24. Charles Moritz, *Current Biography Yearbook 1986* (Bronx, NY: H.W. Wilson Co., 1987), 13.

25. Smith, 12, 15.

26. *Nigger*, 10, 50–66.

27. "Overcrowded, Students Protest in St. Louis." *The Chicago Defender* (National edition) (1921–1967), 29 September 1951.

28. *Callus on My Soul*, 20.

29. *Nigger*, 70, 76.

30. Arthur Steuer, "The Space for Race in Humor," *Esquire Magazine*, November 1961.

31. *Callus on My Soul*, 22.

32. *Nigger*, 83–84.

33. Ibid., 91.

34. *Callus on My Soul*, 27.

35. Smith, 22.

36. Lisa Levenstein, *A Movement Without Marches: African American Women and the Politics of Poverty in Postwar Philadelphia* (Chapel Hill, NC: The University of North Carolina Press, 2009), 133–38.

37. Navy History & Heritage Command, "William Henry 'Bill' Cosby, Jr. (1937–)," *Biographies in Naval History*, http://www.history.navy.mil/bios/cosby_bill.htm.

38. Bill Cosby, *Why Is There Air?* (Burbank, CA: Warner Bros. Records, Inc., 1965).

39. Lawrence Mintz, "Standup Comedy as Social and Cultural Mediation," *American Quarterly* 37, no. 1 (Spring 1985): 78.

40. *Callus on My Soul*, 26.

41. Late Night with Jimmy Fallon, "The Man, The Legend: Bill Cosby," *Late Night with Jimmy Fallon* video, part 1, 9:45, January 19, 2012, http://www.latenightwithjimmyfallon.com/blogs/2012/01/the-man-the-legend-bill-cosby/.

42. Navy History & Heritage Command.

43. Smith, 26.

44. Ibid., 27.

45. Navy History & Heritage Command.

46. Smith, 26.
47. Late Night With Jimmy Fallon.
48. Smith, 29.

Chapter 2

1. "Comedians: Humor, Integrated," *Time Magazine*, February 17, 1961.
2. Alex Dreier, liner notes to *In Living Black & White*, by Dick Gregory (Itasca, IL: Rhino Entertainment Company, 2008; originally published in 1961).
3. Dick Gregory, *In Living Black & White* (Itasca, IL: Rhino Entertainment Company, 2008; originally published in 1961).
4. Thomas Lask, "New Point of View Among Comics," *New York Times*, May 14, 1961, X19.
5. Awards & Shows, "Grammy Awards 1964," http://www.awardsandshows.com/features/grammy-awards-1964-216.html.
6. Allan Sherman, liner notes to *Bill Cosby Is A Very Funny Fellow, Right!* (New York, NY: Warner Brothers, 1963).
7. Richard F. Shepard. "'Big Names' at President's Show Include One Lyndon B. Johnson," *New York Times*, May 23, 1964, 13.
8. Robert Chalmers, "Dick Gregory: Mr. Incredible," *The Independent*, December 19, 2004.
9. "Dick Gregory," *Ebony*, 70.
10. *Nigger*, 90.
11. Ibid., 91.
12. Ibid., 102.
13. Ibid., 105–6.
14. Display Ad 43—No Title, *Chicago Defender*, June 30, 1958.
15. *Nigger*, 111.
16. Ibid.
17. "C and C Sets Turkey Party," *Chicago Defender*, November 27, 1958, 19.
18. Display Ad 14—No Title, *Chicago Defender*, December 24, 1958.
19. "Stars Galore for the Apex Club In Robbins," *Chicago Defender*, January 21, 1959, 19.
20. "Club Apex Offers Hit Acts, Fine Music, Food," *Chicago Defender*, March 10, 1959, 18.
21. "Dick Gregory Stars in Apex Club Show," *Chicago Defender*, June 10, 1959, 18.
22. *Nigger*, 118, 120.
23. Ibid., 120.
24. "Cafes Offer Food on the 'Home' Plan," *Chicago Defender*, September 7, 1959, 19.

25. "Ole Nosey, Snooping as Usual, Hits a Jackpot," *Chicago Defender*, July 9, 1955, 19.

26. *Nigger*, 130.

27. Mel Watkins, *On the Real Side: A History of African American Comedy* (New York, NY: Simon & Schuster, 1994), 82.

28. Bethany Parker, "Probing Question: What Are the Roots of Stand-Up Comedy?," *Penn State News*, last modified September 12, 2008, http://news.psu.edu/story/141330/2008/09/12/research/probing-question-what-are-roots-stand-comedy.

29. *On The Real Side*, 152.

30. Gilbert Millstein, "A Negro Says It With Jokes," *New York Times*, April 30, 1961, SM34.

31. *On the Real Side*, 501.

32. Dotan Oliar and Christopher Sprigman, "There's No Free Laugh (Anymore): The Emergence of Intellectual Property Norms and the Transformation of Stand-Up Comedy," *Virginia Law Review* 94, no. 8 (December 2008): 1793.

33. Gerald Nachman, *Seriously Funny: The Rebel Comedians of the 1950s and 1960s* (New York, NY: Pantheon Books, 2003), 49.

34. Herbert Mitgang, "Anyway, Onward With Mort Sahl," *New York Times*, February 8, 1959, SM32.

35. *In Living Black & White*.

36. *Nigger*, 134–35.

37. Jack Gould, "TV: Discrimination Hit: 'Cast the First Stone,' on A.B.C., Deals with Racial Bias on National Scale," *New York Times*, September 28, 1960, 79.

38. Hugh Hefner, introduction to *From the Back of the Bus*, by Dick Gregory (New York, NY: Avon Books, 1966), 14.

39. Dick Gregory, "Interview of Dick Gregory," interview by Dr. Camille O. Cosby, *National Visionary Leadership Project* (April 29, 2002): 88.

40. Gordon, "Humor in African American Discourse," 274.

41. Steuer, "The Space for Race in Humor."

42. *In Living Black & White*.

43. Chalmers, "Dick Gregory: Mr. Incredible."

44. Joseph Mancini, "Senate Probe Headlines Dick Gregory," *New York Post*, October 28, 1962.

45. Dave Hepburn, "Dick Gregory's Rags-to-Riches Break Good for Half a Million," *New York Amsterdam News*, June 2, 1962, 38.

46. Nat Hentoff, "Goodbye Mistah Bones," *Show Business Illustrated* (October 17, 1961): 94.

47. *Nigger*, 132.

48. Smith, 35.

49. "'Raceless' Bill Cosby," 135.

50. Smith, 36.

51. Ibid., 36–37.

52. Paul Gardner, "Comic Turns Quips into Tuition," *New York Times*, June 25, 1962.

53. Smith, 38–39.

54. Gardner, "Comic Turns Quips into Tuition."

55. "'Raceless' Bill Cosby," 131.

56. "Richard Buckley Dies: Entertainer, 54, Was Known as the Hip Messiah," *New York Times*, November 13, 1960.

57. Smith, 42.

58. "New Negro Comic Draws Writer's Rave," *Chicago Defender*, June 28, 1962, 21.

59. Smith, 46.

60. *Bill Cosby Is A Very Funny Fellow, Right!*

61. Smith, 46–47.

62. Ibid.

63. "Rising Comic Just Wants to Be Funny," *Chicago Defender*, April 23, 1963, 16.

64. "Dick Gregory's Rags-to-Riches Break Good for Half a Million."

65. Brian Ward, *Just My Soul Responding: Rhythm and Blues, Black Consciousness and Race Relations* (Berkeley, CA: University of California Press, 1998).

66. Hilda See, "TV Tapes," *Chicago Defender*, March 14, 1961.

67. Steuer, "The Space for Race in Humor."

68. "Bob Hope Praises Comic's Hot Line," *Chicago Defender*, February 11, 1961, 19.

69. Arthur Gelb, "Comic Withers Prejudice Cliches," *New York Times*, March 20, 1961, 34.

70. "Dick Gregory: New Star Makes Customers Laugh at Integrated Humor," *Ebony*, May 1, 1961, 68.

71. "Comics 'Best' Yesterday or Today? Take Your Pick," *Chicago Defender*, November 29, 1961, 16.

72. Masco Young, "Making Rounds With Top Stars, Combos and Bands," *Chicago Defender*, August 12, 1961, 10.

73. Millstein, "A Negro Says It With Jokes," 34, 37.

74. Howard Taubman, "Adorning the News: Wry Comment Enlivens Informal Theatre," *New York Times*, June 18, 1961, X1.

75. "More Honors for Dick Gregory Comic Socko," *Chicago Defender*, December 4, 1961, 16.

76. "'Comic-of-Year' Dick Gregory Honored by AJ Congress Women," *Jackson Advocate*, January 27, 1962.

77. Nick Lapole, "Dick Gregory Is Great," *New York Journal-American*, April 13, 1962.

78. Joseph Mancini, "Senate Probe Headlines Dick Gregory," *New York Post*, October 28, 1962.

79. Millstein, "A Negro Says It With Jokes."
80. Hentoff, "Goodbye Mistah Bones," 89, 94.
81. Al Monroe, "So They Say," *Chicago Defender*, March 16, 1961, 20.
82. Jesse H. Walker, "Theatricals," *New York Amsterdam News*, February 25, 1961.
83. Gardner, "Comic Turns Quips into Tuition."
84. "New Negro Comic Draws Writer's Rave."

Chapter 3

1. Dick Gregory, "Dick Gregory: The Civil Rights Movement—Part 2" (video of interview by Dr. Camille O. Cosby, *National Visionary Leadership Project*, April 29, 2002), https://www.youtube.com/watch?v=hVtDylZLE-g.
2. Larry Glenn, "Bill Cosby: The Clown As Straight Man," *Tuesday Magazine*, October 1965, 28.
3. Lance Hill, *The Deacons for Defense: Armed Resistance and the Civil Rights Movement* (Chapel Hill: University of North Carolina Press, 2004), 217.
4. "Launch Chicago Food Drive to Aid Starving Miss. Families," *Chicago Defender*, February 2, 1963, 2.
5. Mississippi Department of Archives and History. "Mississippi State Sovereignty Commission: Report by Tom Scarbrough." February 13, 1963, 2.
6. *Nigger*, 160.
7. John Dittmer, *Local People: The Struggle for Civil Rights in Mississippi* (Champaign: University of Illinois Press, 1995), 3.
8. Dick Gregory, liner notes to *My Brother's Keeper*, by Dick Gregory (Pittsburgh, PA: Gateway Recordings, 1963).
9. Dick Gregory, *My Brother's Keeper* (Pittsburgh, PA: Gateway Recordings, 1963).
10. "10,000 Gregory Records to Help Mississippians," *Atlanta Daily World*, March 24, 1963, A1.
11. "Comic's Racial Actions Cited in Magazine Story," *Chicago Defender*, March 27, 1963, 17.
12. Dave Hepburn, "In The Wings: Dick Knows Hunger," *New York Amsterdam*, March 30, 1963, 16.
13. Ted Poston, "Dick Gregory: Not Only Laughter," *New York Post*, April 14, 1963, 2.
14. "Gregory Announces Food Drive for Mississippians," *Atlanta Daily World*, February 6, 1963, 2.
15. *Local People*, 19.
16. Mississippi Department of Archives and History, "Mississippi State Sovereignty Commission: Report by Tom Scarbrough," February 13, 1963, 2.

17. "Goal of 50,000 Pounds of Relief Food for Miss. Farm Workers," *Chicago Defender*, February 7, 1963, 4.

18. "Launch Chicago Food Drive to Aid Starving Miss. Families."

19. "Goal of 50,000 Pounds of Relief Food for Miss. Farm Workers."

20. "Gregory Helps Distribute Chicago Food to Mississippi's Destitute." *Chicago Defender*, February 13, 1963, 3.

21. "Rev. King Issues Food Plea for Miss. Needy," *Chicago Defender*, February 18, 1963, 4.

22. 30,000 More Pounds of Food to Go to Mississippi Friday," *Chicago Defender*, February 14, 1963, 3.

23. "Dixie Chief Calls Food Plan Stunt," *Chicago Defender*, February 16, 1963, 1.

24. Mississippi Department of Archives and History, "Mississippi State Sovereignty Commission: Report by Tom Scarbrough," April 19, 1963, 1.

25. *Nigger*, 162.

26. Mississippi Department of Archives and History, "Mississippi State Sovereignty Commission: Report by Tom Scarbrough," April 4, 1963, 4.

27. " 'No Cadillacking About': Negro Editor Challenges King to Make Himself a Martyr," *Jackson Daily News*, July 6, 1961.

28. "Mississippi State Sovereignty Commission: Report by Tom Scarbrough," April 4, 1963, 4.

29. *Nigger*, 177.

30. "Dick Gregory a One-Man NAACP," *Chicago Defender*, February 5, 1963, 13.

31. "Meredith to Stay at Ole Miss. Gregory Feels," *Chicago Defender*, January 24, 1963, 2.

32. "Gregory Plays Midwife to Meredith's Decision," *Chicago Defender*, January 29, 1963, 13.

33. "Meredith to Stay at Ole Miss. Gregory Feels."

34. "Negro Renewing Try for College," *Commercial Appeal*, December 11, 1958, 57.

35. "Negro Reports Good Advice on College Plans," *Hattiesburg American*, January 6, 1959.

36. Mississippi Department of Archives and History, Memorandum [SCR ID # 1-27-0-26-1-1-1], August 27, 1959.

37. "Negro Is Arrested at MSC," *State Times*, September 15, 1959.

38. "Negro Is Jailed After Attempt to Enroll in Southern Classes," *Clarion Ledger*, September 16, 1959.

39. Mississippi Department of Archives and History [SCR ID # 1-27-0-68-1-1-1], January 27, 1963.

40. *Nigger*, 159.

41. "Freed but Dying Kennard May Come to Hospital," *Chicago Defender*, January 30, 1963, 3.

42. "Clyde Kennard Dies in Chicago Hospital," *Jackson Daily News*, July 5, 1963.

43. Timothy J. Minchond and John A. Salmond, "'The Saddest Story of the Whole Movement': The Clyde Kennard Case and the Search for Racial Reconciliation in Mississippi, 1955–2007," *Journal of Mississippi History* 71, no. 3 (Fall 2009): 193.

44. Milton Esterow, "Dick Gregory Comes Marching In," *New York Times*, September 9, 1963.

45. "Dick Gregory Comes Marching In."

46. "In The Wings: Dick Knows Hunger."

47. James A. Wechsler, "The Tragedian," *New York Post*, May 8, 1963.

48. "Gregory Vows to Carry On in Greenwood," *New York Post*, April 4, 1963.

49. "Gregory Spends $60,000 on Racial Causes," *Chicago Defender*, March 12, 1963, 13.

50. Alfred T. Hendricks, "Dick Gregory Is Fired by Queens Club," *New York Post*, April 17, 1963.

51. "Dick Gregory a One-Man NAACP."

52. Ole Nosey, "Everybody Goes When the Wagon Comes," *Chicago Defender*, February 9, 1963, 10.

53. "Dick Gregory Leads March On Restaurants," *Atlanta Daily World*, January 1, 1964, 1.

54. "Accord Ends Ga. Sit-Ins," *New York Amsterdam*, January 18, 1964, 29.

55. Patrick Harden, "Dobbs, Toddle Integrated in Southern Cities," *Atlanta Daily World*, January 15, 1964, 4.

56. Eric Foner, *Give Me Liberty!: An American History*, vol. II, 3rd ed. (New York: W.W. Norton & Co., 2012), 956–57.

57. "Chicago Comic's Racial Humor," *Jet Magazine*, March 9, 1961, 60.

58. "Gregory Held in Arkansas," *New York Times*, February 18, 1964, 21.

59. Emily Raymond, *Stars for Freedom: Hollywood, Black Celebrities, and the Civil Rights Movement* (Seattle, WA: University of Washington Press, 2015), 149.

60. "Dick Gregory Threatens Md. With '40 Days.'" *Chicago Defender*, March 5, 1964, 29.

61. M. Wilson Lewis. "Civil Rights Leaders Form New, Militant '3rd Force.'" *Chicago Defender*, March 21, 1964, 1.

62. "Dick Gregory Shot in L.A. Riot," *New York Post*, August 13, 1965.

63. Drew Pearson, "Gregory and the Riot," *New York Post*, August 18, 1965.

64. "Dick Gregory Shot in Leg; Riots Flare Again in L.A.," *New York World-Telegram*, August 13, 1965, 2.

65. "Ossie Davis' Stirring Tribute to Malcolm X," *New York Amsterdam*, March 6, 1965, 1.

66. Milton Esterow, "End Papers: NIGGER. An Autobiography by Dick Gregory with Robert Lipsyte," *New York Times*, October 15, 1964, 37.

67. *Nigger*, dedication page.

68. Joseph Watkins Jr, "Dick Gregory Top Notch Negro Leader," *Chicago Defender*, May 16, 1964, 9.

69. Dave Hepburn. "In The Wings: The Rumor Mill," *New York Amsterdam*, August 22, 1964, 14.

70. *Bill Cosby Is a Very Funny Fellow, Right!*

71. "Rising Comic Just Wants to Be Funny," *Chicago Defender*, April 20, 1963, 19.

72. "Riiight." *Newsweek*, June 17, 1963.

73. *Cosby*, 51.

74. Ibid.

75. Aram Goudsouzian, *Sidney Poitier: Man, Actor, Icon* (Chapel Hill: University of North Carolina Press, 2003), 112.

76. "Life With Bill Cosby," *Ebony*, September 1, 1966, 34.

77. *Cosby*, 57.

78. Jesse H. Walker, "Theatricals," *New York Amsterdam*, December 14, 1963, 17.

79. "A Very Young Bill Cosby on the Jack Paar Show," VideoSift, Flash video file, http://videosift.com/video/A-Very-Young-Bill-Cosby-on-The-Jack-Paar-Show.

80. "Bill Cosby: Variety Is the Life of Spies," 88.

81. Bill Cosby, *I Started Out as a Child* (Burbank, CA: Warner Bros., 1964).

82. Smith, 59.

83. Helen Dudar, "Bill Cosby: Up From the Cellar." *New York Post*, February 23, 1964, 31.

84. Lillian S. Calhoun, "Fast-Rising Comedian Bill Cosby Talks About His Different Approach to Comedy." *Chicago Defender*, August 1, 1964, 4.

85. Ibid.

86. "More Cities Added in NAACP TV Spectacular," *New York Amsterdam*, May 9, 1964, 63.

87. Robert de Roos, "The Spy Who Came in for the Gold," *TV Guide*, October 23, 1965, 14–15.

88. "Bill Cosby: Variety Is the Life of Spies," 88.

89. "Cosby to Appear in TV Spy Series," *New York Times*, November 16, 1964, 63.

90. Paul Gardner, "Ethical Culture Unit Assails Attitude of TV Toward Negro," *New York Times*, December 7, 1964, 71.

91. Jesse H. Walker, "Theatricals," *New York Amsterdam*, January 9, 1965, 15.

92. Donald Bogle, *Prime Time Blues: African Americans on Network Television* (New York, NY: Farrar Straus Giroux, 2001), 42.

93. Dave Hepburn, "In The Wings," *New York Amsterdam*, August 15, 1964, 16.

94. Glenn, "Bill Cosby: The Clown as Straight Man," 28.

95. De Roos, "The Spy Who Came in for the Gold," 16.

96. Louie Robinson, "The Pleasures and Problems of Being Bill Cosby," *Ebony*, July 1, 1969, 146, 148.

97. Glenn, "Bill Cosby: The Clown as Straight Man," 28.

98. De Roos, "The Spy Who Came in for the Gold."

99. Glenn, "Bill Cosby: The Clown as Straight Man," 28.

100. Joanne Stang, "The Case of the Scholarly 'Spy,'" *New York Times*, October 17, 1965, 21.

101. "Bill Cosby: Variety Is the Life of Spies," *Saturday Evening Post*, September 25, 1965, 86.

102. Jesse H. Walker, "Theatricals," *New York Amsterdam*, October 2, 1965, 22.

103. James L. Hicks, "'I Spy' a Negro Hero," *New York Amsterdam*, October 2, 1965, 17.

104. Stan Cornyn, liner notes to *Why Is There Air?* by Bill Cosby (Burbank, CA: Warner Bros., 1965).

105. Jesse H. Walker, "Theatricals," *New York Amsterdam*, January 16, 1965, 15.

Chapter 4

1. *Callus on My Soul*, 127.

2. See Mark Lane and Dick Gregory, *Murder in Memphis: The FBI and the Assassination of Martin Luther King* (New York: Thunder's Mouth Press, 1977); originally titled *Code Name Zorro*.

3. Robert Lipsyte, *An Accidental Sportswriter: A Memoir* (New York: Harper-Collins, 2011), 53.

4. Thomas A. Johnson, "Dick Gregory Going to Hanoi to Arrange Shows for G.I. Captives," *New York Times*, December 4, 1966.

5. "Dick Gregory in the Hospital—He Persists in Hunger Strike," *New York Post*, July 5, 1968, 14.

6. "Mississippi State Sovereignty Commission: Memo by Fred McRackin," File SCR ID # 2-112-2-53-1-1-1, December 15, 1967.

7. Dick Gregory, *Write Me In!* (New York: Bantam Books, 1968), 48.

8. *Cosby*, 74–75.

9. Bill Cosby, *Revenge* (Burbank, CA: 1998); originally released in 1967.

10. Arthur Whitman, "Bill Cosby: The Spy Who Knocked 'Em Cold," *True: The Man's Magazine* 48, no. 356 (January 1967): 80.

11. Florabel Muir, "A Million Disks," *New York Daily News,* February 10, 1967, 72.

12. *Cosby*, 85.

13. Gene Roberts, "Mississippi Reduces Police Protection for Marchers," *New York Times*, June 17, 1966, 1.

14. *Callus on My Soul*, 113.

15. *Nigger*, 157.

16. John Kifner, "Rights Leaders Plan to Take Up Meredith's March in Mississippi," *New York Times*, June 7, 1966, 28.

17. "Meredith Is Wounded by Shotgun Blasts," *Chicago Defender*, June 7, 1966, 2–3.

18. "Aubrey Norvell Pleads Guilty, Sentenced," *Daytona Beach Morning Journal*, November 22, 1966.

19. "Huge Mississippi March to Follow Meredith Attack," *Chicago Defender*, June 8, 1966, 2.

20. *Nigger*, 205.

21. *Dick Gregory Talks Turkey*.

22. Aram Goudsouzian, *Down to the Crossroads: Civil Rights, Black Power, and the Meredith March Against Fear* (New York: Farrar, Straus and Giroux, 2014), 31.

23. Gregory, *Callus on My Soul*, 114.

24. "Oakland Group Makes Charges of Police Brutality," *Chicago Defender*, June 14, 1966, 4; Goudsouzian, *Down to the Crossroads*, 215.

25. Gene Roberts, "Troopers Shove Group Resuming Meredith March," *New York Times*, June 8, 1966, 2.

26. Peniel Joseph, *Waiting 'Til the Midnight Hour: A Narrative History of Black Power in America* (New York: Holt and Co., 2006), 138.

27. "Rights Leaders Plan to Take Up Meredith's March in Mississippi," 28; Neil A. Maxwell, "Militancy on the March: Non-Violence Is Fast Losing Favor as a Civil Rights Tool," *Wall Street Journal*, 8.

28. "Rights Leaders Plan to Take Up Meredith's March in Mississippi," 28.

29. *Down to the Crossroads*, 214.

30. "Rights Leaders Plan to Take Up Meredith's March in Mississippi," 28.

31. Gordon Parks, "Whip of Black Power," *Life Magazine*, May 19, 1967, 79.

32. Oral History Interview with John Lewis, November 20, 1973, Interview A-0073, Southern Oral History Program Collection (#4007) in the Southern Oral History Program Collection, Southern Historical Collection, Wilson Library, University of North Carolina at Chapel Hill.

33. Gene Roberts, "Meredith Leads the March on Eve of Rally in Jackson," *New York Times*, June 26, 1966, 40; Oral History Interview with John Lewis.

34. William Van Deburg, *New Day in Babylon: The Black Power Movement and American Culture, 1965–1975* (Chicago, IL: University of Chicago Press, 1993), 126.

35. Martin Luther King Jr., "Statement on Black Power" (statement released by the Southern Christian Leadership Conference, October 14, 1966).

36. Fred Wright, "Dick Gregory: Compelling Orator With Cause," *Evening Independent*, April 14, 1971, Section B.

37. Roy Reed, "Meredith Flies Home After Fainting in Hospital," *New York Times*, June 9, 1966, 32.

Notes to Chapter 4

38. Adolph J. Slaughter, "The Slaughter Pen: Aftermath of 'Meredith's Folly,'" *Chicago Defender*, July 2, 1966, 2.
39. Mississippi Department of Archives and History, Folder SCR ID # 9-31-5-41-1-1-1, June 15, 1966, 1.
40. James Coleman, "An Oral History with James C. Coleman," Interview by Harriet Tanzman, Tougaloo College Archives, April 12, 2000.
41. "Civil Rights Chiefs Close Ranks Behind Meredith," *Toledo Blade*, June 26, 1966, 1.
42. "An Oral History with James C. Coleman."
43. Mississippi Department of Archives and History, "Rally for Meredith March," WLBT Newsfilm Collection, Reel D47, LCN 181, June 25, 1966.
44. Slaughter, "The Slaughter Pen: Aftermath of 'Meredith's Folly,'" 2.
45. Charles Evers, Interview by Author, Phone, Jackson, MS, May 29, 2014.
46. *CBS News*, "Black Power, White Backlash," September 27, 1966.
47. Ibid.
48. *Down to the Crossroads*, 253.
49. Joe Flaherty, "Dick Gregory on His Way to Entertain the Jailed," *Village Voice* XII, no. 8, December 8, 1966.
50. Drew Pearson, "Dick Gregory in Race?," *New York Post*, February 27, 1966.
51. Robert Lipsyte, "You Gits a Little Uppity and You Lands in Jail," *Esquire*, August 1967, 75.
52. Pearson, "Dick Gregory in Race?"
53. Robert Davis, "Washington Elected: City Has First Black Mayor," *Chicago Tribune*, April 12, 1983, 1.
54. Elliot Asinof, "Dick Gregory Is Not So Funny Now," *New York Times Magazine*, March 17, 1968, 50.
55. "You Gits a Little Uppity and You Lands in Jail," 74; "Dick Gregory Is Not So Funny Now," 47.
56. Archer Winsten, "Rages and Outrages," *New York Post*, January 23, 1967, 24.
57. "Dick Gregory Is Not So Funny Now," 45, 47.
58. Display Ad 26, *Chicago Defender*, November 4, 1968, 11.
59. *Write Me In!*, 14.
60. Ibid., 68, 75.
61. "1968 Presidential General Election Results," US Election Atlas, http://uselectionatlas.org/RESULTS/national.php?year=1968.
62. "Dick Gregory Is Not So Funny Now," 52.
63. "Master Mimic Bill Cosby: An Electronic Mark Twain," *Life Magazine*, March 15, 1968, 40.
64. "Color Him Funny," *Newsweek*, January 31, 1966, 76.
65. "Master Mimic Bill Cosby: An Electronic Mark Twain," 37.
66. *Cosby*, 77.

67. See the Forethought of W.E.B. Du Bois, *Souls of Black Folk* (New York: Dover Publications, 1994), v; originally published in 1903. Du Bois states, "Herein lie buried many things which if read with patience may show the strange meaning of being black here in the dawn of the Twentieth Century. This meaning is not without interest to you, Gentle Reader; for the problem of the Twentieth Century is the problem of the color-line."

68. "Master Mimic Bill Cosby: An Electronic Mark Twain," 38.

69. Joan Barthel, "Cosby: 'Boom, That's It, Goodbye,'" *New York Times*, March 17, 1968, 24.

70. "Color Him Funny," 76.

71. "Bill Cosby: The Spy Who Knocked 'Em Cold," 81.

72. "Cosby: 'Boom, That's It, Goodbye,'" 32.

73. For more on the death of Richard Claxton Gregory Jr., see *Nigger*, 182–87.

74. "Cosby: 'Boom, That's It, Goodbye,'" 24.

75. Tom Burke, "It Pays to Be Flip," *New York Times*, October 13, 1968, D27.

76. "Godfrey Cambridge Signed by C.B.S.-TV to 10-Year Contract," *New York Times*, July 10, 1968, 79.

77. "Beyond Laughter," *Ebony Magazine*, September 1967, 90.

78. "Color Him Funny," 76.

79. "Master Mimic Bill Cosby: An Electronic Mark Twain," 37.

80. Barbara Delatiner, "Cosby's Humor Needs a City Ear," *Newsday*, January 19, 1968.

81. "Color Him Funny," 76.

82. "Bill Cosby: The Spy Who Knocked 'Em Cold," 81.

83. Bill Cosby, *To Russell, My Brother, Whom I Slept With* (Burbank, CA: Warner Bros. Records, Inc., 1998); originally published in 1968.

84. J. M. Flagler, "A Spy Off Duty," *Look Magazine*, May 30, 1967, M21.

85. "Bill Cosby: The Spy Who Knocked 'Em Cold," 81.

86. "Color Him Funny," 76.

87. Joanne Stang, "Cosby Promised His Teacher He'd Never Sing 'Old Black Joe' Again," *New York Times*, June 30, 1968, D17.

88. *Black History: Lost, Stolen or Strayed*, DVD, narrated by Bill Cosby (St. Louis, MO: Phoenix Learning Group, Inc., 2008); originally aired in 1968.

89. Ibid.

Chapter 5

1. Michael McGuire, "Dick Gregory to Talk with N. Viets in Paris," *Chicago Tribune*, November 29, 1969, Section 1, 8.

2. Jack Gould, "TV: The Return of Two N.B.C. Season Highlights," *New York Times*, September 12, 1969, 87.

3. Dick Gregory, *Dick Gregory: The Light Side: The Dark Side* (Narbeth, PA: Collectables, 1997; originally released in 1969).

4. Donald Mosby, "Despite Guard, Cops, Federal Troops, More Looting Hits Ghetto," *Chicago Defender*, April 8, 1968, 1.

5. Thomas Powers, "Report: 9 Slain in Rioting; 3,000 Guardsmen Patrolling Streets, Daley Pleads for an End to Violence, Urges Show of Pride by Chicagoans," *Chicago Tribune*, April 6, 1968, 1, col. 3; *The Light Side: The Dark Side*.

6. Edward Schreiber, "Shoot Arsonists: Daley; Appoints Committee to Investigate Riots," *Chicago Tribune*, April 16, 1968, 1, col. 4.

7. "Negroes Express Concern, Dismay At Daley's Order," *The Blade*, April 16, 1968, 1.

8. Leon F. Litwack, *Trouble in Mind: Black Southerners in the Age of Jim Crow* (New York: Alfred A. Knopf, 1998), 332.

9. *The Light Side: The Dark Side.*

10. Carlyle C. Douglas, "Diogenes, Put Down Your Lamp!: In Dick Gregory, the World Has Found an Honest Man," *Ebony*, April 1970, 74; "Here He Is, Folks, Dick Gregory: Fizz, Crackle, Zap, Ba-Room," 42.

11. Lindsay Patterson, "Gregory Talking Back," *New York Times*, September 7, 1969, Section D, 40.

12. Tom Mackin, "Dick Gregory Up Tight," *Evening News*, January 5, 1970, 15.

13. Jack Gould, "TV: Dick Gregory Speaks Out at U. of Alabama," *New York Times*, January 6, 1970, 83.

14. "Power Failure Cut Gregory in Chicago," *New York Times*, January 8, 1970, 78.

15. "Entertainment: Station Apologizes for Cutting Off Gregory Show," *Jet*, January 22, 1970, 58.

16. See James Meriwether, *Proudly We Can Be Africans: Black Americans and Africa, 1935–1961* (Chapel Hill, NC: University of North Carolina Press, 2002); Brenda Gayle Plummer, *In Search of Power: African Americans in the Era of Decolonization, 1956–1974* (New York, NY: Cambridge University Press, 2012).

17. Kwame Nimako, "Nkrumah, African Awakening and Neo-colonialism: How Black America Awakened Nkrumah and Nkrumah Awakened Black America," *The Black Scholar* 40, no. 2 (Summer 2010): 55.

18. Kwame Nkrumah, *Ghana: The Autobiography of Kwame Nkrumah* (New York: International Publishers, 1957), 45.

19. "Nkrumah, African Awakening and Neo-colonialism," 62, 67–68.

20. P. L. Prattis, "Ghana and Us," *Pittsburgh Courier*, March 23, 1957, 8; Kevin Gaines, *American Africans in Ghana: Black Expatriates and the Civil Rights Era* (Chapel Hill, NC: University of North Carolina Press, 2008).

21. "Denied Australian Visa, Gregory Says 'Who's Funny?,'" *Jet*, September 24, 1970, 56.
22. "Two Gregory Children on Extended African Tour," *Jet*, September 3, 1970, 42.
23. *Callus on My Soul*, 171.
24. "Bar Greg From Australian Visit," *Chicago Defender*, September 3, 1970, 36.
25. *Callus on My Soul*, 171–72.
26. "Dick Gregory Denied Visit to Australia," *New York Amsterdam News*, September 12, 1970, 35.
27. Maximilian Walsh, "Australia Veers Right," *Christian Science Monitor*, September 4, 1970.
28. "Greets Gregory," *Jet*, October 8, 1970, 47.
29. "Dick Gregory Talks Up Giant Cabal in Which Assassinations Are Linked," *Variety*, April 9, 1969, 2.
30. "Genocide Petition Filed Against U.S.," *New York Amsterdam*, July 4, 1970, 43.
31. Blacks and Puerto Ricans Bid U.N. Act on 'Genocide,'" *New York Times*, November 17, 1970, 16.
32. Roger M. Williams, "Dick Gregory: From Stand-Up Comic to Lie-Down Martyr," *World*, August 15, 1972, 22.
33. Dick Gregory, "Can Black and White Artists Still Work Together?," *New York Times*, February 2, 1969, D1.
34. "Here He Is, Folks, Dick Gregory."
35. "Return of the Native Son," *Newsweek*, June 29, 1970, 74.
36. Ibid.
37. Stanford University, "Letter from Birmingham Jail," Martin Luther King Jr. Papers Project, http://mlk-kpp01.stanford.edu/kingweb/liberation_curriculum/pdfs/letterfrombirmingham_wwcw.pdf.
38. "Gregory Talking Back," 40D.
39. "Dick Gregory: Career Does a Turnaround," 9C.
40. "Here He Is, Folks, Dick Gregory: Fizz, Crackle, Zap, Ba-Room," 42.
41. *Callus on My Soul*, 173.
42. Alfred G. Aronowitz, "Gregory, Brain Surgeon," *New York Post*, June 10, 1970, 91.
43. "Dick Gregory: From Stand-Up Comic to Lie-Down Martyr," 20.
44. "Dick Gregory: Career Does a Turnaround," 9C.
45. "Diogenes, Put Down Your Lamp!: In Dick Gregory, the World Has Found an Honest Man," 81.
46. "Dick Gregory: From Stand-Up Comic to Lie-Down Martyr," 21.
47. *Callus on My Soul*, 124, 20.
48. "Gregory, Brain Surgeon," 91.

49. Arthur Hirsch, "Back on the Laugh Track, A Comic Returns: Dick Gregory, Once Ahead of His Time, Is Catching Up With Himself," *Baltimore Sun*, November 29, 1995, http://articles.baltimoresun.com/1995-11-29/features/1995333033_1_dick-gregory-gregory-live-gregory-notes.

50. "Return of the Native Son," 74.

51. "Dick Gregory: From Stand-Up Comic to Lie-Down Martyr," 24.

52. Ibid., 23.

53. "Gregory Returning Home After Being Released From Jail," *Chicago Defender*, July 18, 1968, 8.

54. "Greg's 40 Day Fast to Score U.S. Drug Ills," *Chicago Defender*, June 15, 1970, 1.

55. "Dick Gregory: From Stand-Up Comic to Lie-Down Martyr," 19.

56. Bryant Rollins, "Gregory Still Fasting and Still Funny," *New York Amsterdam*, June 24, 1972, D1.

57. "Shorter Reviews," *New York Times*, May 13, 1973, 378.

58. Lesley Crosson, "A New Leaf," *New York Amsterdam*, December 15, 1973, D10.

59. "We Plan Dick Gregory Day Salute," *Chicago Defender*, November 15, 1973, 16.

60. Peter Coutrous, "Here He Is, Folks, Dick Gregory: Fizz, Crackle, Zap, Ba-Room," *Daily News*, June 22, 1970, 42.

61. Earl Calloway, "Stars and Youth Pay Tribute to Gregory," *Chicago Defender*, December 1, 1973, 18.

62. Peter Benchley, "Dick Gregory: Career Does a Turnaround," *Hartford Times*, July 19, 1970, 9C.

63. *Callus on My Soul*, 177.

64. Ibid., 176, 187; "Ali Credits Dick Gregory Formula for His Energy," *Jet*, October 12, 1978, 23.

65. *Callus on My Soul*, 177.

66. Gerald Nachman, "Bill Cosby: Football's Loss," *New York Post*, July 1967, Section 3.

67. Donald Bogle, *Prime Time Blues: African Americans on Network Television* (New York, NY: Farrar, Straus, and Giroux, 2001), 140–42.

68. Bob Thomas, "Stars Diahann Carroll: New Series Causes Talk," *Austin Statesman*, May 31, 1968, 38.

69. Richard Warren Lewis, "The Importance of Being Julia," *TV Guide*, December 14, 1968, 26.

70. *Prime Time Blues*, 151.

71. "Bill Cosby Forms Own Omnibus Company," *Jet*, June 26, 1969, 55.

72. "Cosby Quits Record Co.; To Manage Acting Career," *Jet*, May 29, 1969, 56.

73. Kay Gardella, "Teacher Role for Cosby Plumbs Human Behavior," *Daily News*, August 12, 1969, 30.

74. Jerry Buck, "Cosby Holds the Reins," *Courier-Journal & Times*, August 10, 1969.

75. "Teacher Role for Cosby Plumbs Human Behavior," 30.

76. *Cosby*, 89.

77. "Teacher Role for Cosby Plumbs Human Behavior," 30.

78. Faith Berry, "Can 'Just for Laughs' Be Real for Blacks?," *New York Times*, December 7, 1969, D23.

79. *Cosby*, 91.

80. A. S. Doc Young, "'Bill Cosby Is Not Malcolm X, He's Bill Cosby,'" *New York Times*, December 21, 1969, D21.

81. Ibid.

82. "Can 'Just for Laughs' Be Real for Blacks?"

83. "Give Us the Children," *Variety*, May 27, 1970, 35.

84. Ibid.

85. Roderick Nordell, "TV: Specials and Specials," *Christian Science Monitor*, November 15, 1969.

86. Howard Thompson, "TV: A Revealing Close-Up of Golda Meier Is Set: A.B.C. Explores World . . . ," *New York Times*, May 5, 1973, 79.

87. "Cosby's 'Fat Albert' to Star in New Children's Series," *New York Amsterdam*, June 19, 1972, D7.

88. Bill Cosby, "An Integration of the Visual Media via *Fat Albert and the Cosby Kids* into the Elementary School Curriculum as a Teaching Aid and Vehicle to Achieve Increased Learning," PhD diss., University of Massachusetts, 1976.

89. Robert Kerwin, "Cosby: The Man, the MA, and the Money," *Leisure*, June 1, 1975, 7.

90. Bob Thomas, "Cosby to Do Clean Films—No Cussing, No Nudity," *New York Post*, June 2, 1971.

91. "Bill Cosby to Finance His Film Debut; $1-Mil Budget, Wants G Tag," *Variety*, October 28, 1970, 2.

92. Kay Gardella, "Cosby's Drama Tonight Aimed at Those Who Care," *Daily News*, February 25, 1972.

93. "Cosby to Do Clean Films—No Cussing, No Nudity."

94. *Sidney Poitier: Man, Actor, Icon*, 355.

95. Mike Stratton. "Bill Cosby on Prejudice (1971)," *YouTube*, Online Video Clip, November 17, 2012; originally published in 1971, http://www.youtube.com/watch?v=z6vMTZZZMqQ.

96. "Dick Gregory: From Stand-Up Comic to Lie-Down Martyr," 19.

Epilogue

1. William Plummer, "After 27 Years in His Bedroom, 1,200-Lb. Walter Hudson Decides to Take a Load Off," *People* 28, no. 17 (October 26, 1987): 60;

"Walter Hudson, Lost 700 Pounds, Dies at Age 46," *Sunday Gazette*, December 25, 1991, D5.

2. Richette L. Haywood, "Inability To Get Up, Go to Mother's Funeral Gives 700-Pounder Will To Diet," *Jet*, October 5, 1987, 54.

3. Plummer, "After 27 Years in His Bedroom," 61.

4. "Ali Credits Dick Gregory Formula for His Energy," 23.

5. Billy Lee with Dick Lally, *The Wrong Stuff* (New York, NY: Viking, 1984), 197–98.

6. "Willie Stargell: Of Course Pop Is Getting Older, but the Pirates Know He's Getting Better Too," *People* 12, no. 26, December 24, 1979, 78.

7. *Callus on My Soul*, 190.

8. "Millions Facing Starvation in Ethiopia; No End in Sight for Drought, Famine," *The Hour*, February 16, 1984, 24.

9. "Activist Dick Gregory Leading Delegation to Fight African Hunger," *Jet*, December 17, 1984, 8.

10. "Dick Gregory's Formula to Be Used All Over Ethiopia Following Successful Tests," *Jet*, May 27, 1985, 13.

11. "Gregory to Market His Slim Safe Diet Here," *New York Amsterdam*, December 8, 1984, 14.

12. "New Dick Gregory Diet Provides Job Opportunities," *Jet*, September 24, 1984, 8.

13. "Dick Gregory's Client Sheds 243 Pounds at His New Weight Loss Center," *Jet*, April 21, 1986, 12.

14. Anemene Hertecellis, "Trip to Clinic Refused; Fat Man Won't Leave Home," *The Bulletin*, February 5, 1988, A3.

15. "Walter Hudson, Lost 700 Pounds, Dies at Age 46," D5.

16. *Callus on My Soul*, 227–28.

17. "Dick Gregory Signs $100 Million Contract," *Afro-American*, October 6, 1984, 6.

18. Howard Manly, "Gregory Buys Hotel and Fattens His Diet Empire," *Black Enterprise*, March 1989, 22; Thomas E. Bennett, "Greenbelt Businessman Helps Dick Gregory Market New Product," *Afro-American*, April 4, 1987, 16.

19. *Callus on My Soul*, 229.

20. George Masnick, Senior Research Fellow at The Harvard Joint Center for Housing Studies, defines Generation X as those born between 1965 and 1984. See Masnick, "Defining the Generations," *The Harvard Joint Center for Housing Studies Blog*, November 28, 2012, http://housingperspectives.blogspot.com/2012/11/defining-generations.html.

21. Tracey Webb, "Dick Gregory Launches D.C.'s Drug Program," *Atlanta Daily World*, February 21, 1991, 6.

22. Abiola Sinclair, "Shocker Evidence Found in Atlanta Child Murders: Famous Lawyer Plans to File an Appeal Soon," *Atlanta Daily World*, January 27, 1990, 1.

23. William Reed, "Blame Laid to Government for Cocaine in Black Neighborhoods?," *Atlanta Daily World*, October 3, 1996, 1.

24. "Dick Gregory Arrested for Disturbing Peace," *Atlanta Daily World*, March 26, 1992, 7; *Callus On My Soul*, 243.

25. Ben Brantley, "Advice From an Authority: Laugh!," *New York Times*, December 15, 1995, C3; "Dick Gregory's back on stage performing . . . ," *Atlanta Daily World*, October 19, 1995, 7.

26. *Callus on My Soul*, 286.

27. Andrew Barker, "Dick Gregory Receives a Star on the Walk of Fame," *Variety*, February 2, 2015, http://variety.com/2015/film/features/dick-gregory-receives-a-star-on-the-walk-of-fame-1201421388.

28. "Bill Cosby Pays Tribute to Dick Gregory," *YouTube*, Online Video Clip, October 2, 2014, https://www.youtube.com/watch?v=utPnb5WLbPk.

29. *Callus on My Soul*, 287.

30. Christopher Rosen, "Stars Mourn Death of Activist and Comedian Dick Gregory," *Entertainment Weekly*, August 20, 2017, http://ew.com/news/2017/08/20/dick-gregory-dead/.

31. "Dick Gregory's Son: Emmys Snub 'Highly Disrespectful' . . . We Never Got a Phone Call," *TMZ*, September 18, 2017.

32. Cosby, Bill. Twitter Post. September 13, 2017. 12:49 p.m., https://twitter.com/BillCosby/status/908024916141907968.

33. Audrey Thomas McCluskey, ed. *Richard Pryor: The Life and Legacy of a "Crazy" Black Man* (Bloomington, IN: Indiana University Press).

34. *Cosby*, 154.

35. John Lippman, "NBC Renews 'Cosby' at Lower Fee," *Los Angeles Times*, May 3, 1991, http://articles.latimes.com/1991-05-03/business/fi-1066_1_cosby-show.

36. *Cosby*, 164–65.

37. Darryl Pinckney, "The Black Face That's a Mirror for Everyone," *New York Times*, September 8, 1996, Section 2, 66.

38. *Cosby*, 165.

39. "The Black Face That's a Mirror for Everyone," 66.

40. "Season 1 Episode 01-Pilot Presentation," *YouTube*. Online Video Clip, September 11, 2007, https://www.youtube.com/watch?v=nFY0HBkUm8o.

41. Ta-Nehisi Coates, "Mushmouth Reconsidered," *Village Voice*, July 14, 2004, 34.

42. Michele Greppi, "Cosby's Complaint: TV's Black Shows Are 'Backward,' " *New York Post*, October 8, 1991, 68.

43. Frank DiGiacomo and Joanna Molloy, with Florence Anthony, "Cosby Rips New Black TV Shows," *New York Post*, October 6, 1992, 6.

44. Harry Stein, "Bill's Broadside at Today's Black Sitcoms Is No Laughing Matter," *TV Guide*, November 7, 1992, 35.

45. Bill Carter, "Bill Cosby Trying to Buy NBC From G.E.," *New York Times*, October 2, 1992, D22.

46. U.S. Department of Justice, Bureau of Justice Statistics, *Homicide Trends in the United States, 1980–2008* by Alexia Cooper and Erica L. Smith, Washington, DC: GPO, 2011, http://www.bjs.gov/content/pub/pdf/htus8008.pdf.

47. Alison Mitchell, "2 Brooklyn High School Students Are Shot to Death Hours Before Visit by Dinkins," *New York Times*, February 27, 1992, A1.

48. Mike Kolenak and Andrea Peyser, "Bill Cosby's Plea to Students: Stop the Killing," *New York Post*, March 3, 1992, 13.

49. Lorin Smith, "Bill Cosby Is Challenging Keynoter at Bermuda Educational Conference," February 26, 1994, 23.

50. Camille Cosby, "A Mother's Call for Healing," *Daily News*, July 9, 1998, 23.

51. Brendan Bourne and Bill Hoffmann, "Mrs. Cosby Says America Taught Her Son's Killer to Hate Blacks," *New York Post*, July 9, 1998, 10; "Ennis' Mom: U.S. Taught Killer Racism," *Newsday*, July 9, 1998, A33; *Cosby*, 233.

52. Jere Hester, "'We've Got to Laugh: Cos Works Through Pain; Wife Craves Justice," *Daily News*, January 27, 1997, 7.

53. "Dr. Bill Cosby Speaks at the 50th Anniversary Commemoration of the *Brown v. Topeka Board of Education* Supreme Court Decision," *Rutgers Computing Services*, http://www.rci.rutgers.edu/~schochet/101/Cosby_Speech.htm.

54. "A Cos for Alarm: the Music Industry," *Newsday*, July 30, 2004, A12.

55. Deborah Solomon, "Bill Cosby's Not Funny," *New York Times*, March 27, 2005, G15.

56. Ta-Nehisi Coates, "'This Is How We Lost to the White Man': The Audacity of Bill Cosby's Black Conservatism," *The Atlantic*, May 2008, http://www.theatlantic.com/magazine/archive/2008/05/-this-is-how-we-lost-to-the-white-man/306774.

57. Jamal E. Watson, "More Tough Love from Cosby," *New York Amsterdam*, July 8–14, 2004, 3.

58. Leonard Pitts Jr., "The Cosby Speech," *am New York*, May 24, 2004, 08.

59. "Key & Peele—East/West College Bowl," *YouTube*. Online Video Clip, September 20, 2012, https://www.youtube.com/watch?v=gODZzSOelss.

60. "Key & Peele—Substitute Teacher," *YouTube*, Online Video Clip, October 17, 2012, https://www.youtube.com/watch?v=Dd7FixvoKBw.

61. Bill Cosby and Alvin F. Poussaint, *Come On People!: On the Path from Victims to Victors* (Nashville, TN: Thomas Nelson, 2007); "The Cosby Crusade," *Wall Street Journal*, May 1, 2009, W4.

62. Daniel Arkin, Andrew Blankstein, and Tom Winter, "Judge Explains Why He Unsealed Bill Cosby Court Documents," July 7, 2015, https://www.nbcnews.com/storyline/bill-cosby-scandal/judge-explains-why-he-unsealed-bill-cosby-court-documents-n387861.

Works Cited

Archival Collections

Carbondale, Illinois
    Morris Library, Southern Illinois University
    Special Collections Research Center, Rip Stokes Photograph Collection
Chapel Hill, North Carolina
    Wilson Library, University of North Carolina
    Southern Historical Collection, Southern Oral History Program Collection
Jackson, Mississippi
    L. Zenobia Coleman Library, Tougaloo College
    Tougaloo College Archives
    Mississippi Department of Archives and History
New York, New York
    New York Public Library for the Performing Arts
    Schomburg Center for Research in Black Culture
Philadelphia, Pennsylvania
    Temple University Libraries
    Charles L. Blockson Afro-American Collection, John W. Mosley Photograph Collection

Private Collection

Everett Collection

Interviews by the Author

Cosby, Bill. Interview via telephone, December 10, 2013.
Evers, Charles. Interview via telephone, May 29, 2014.

Works Cited

Newspapers and Periodicals

Afro-American
AM New York
Atlanta Daily World
Austin Statesman
The Atlantic
Baltimore Sun
Black Enterprise
The Blade
The Bulletin
Chicago Defender
Chicago Tribune
Christian Science Monitor
Clarion Ledger
Commercial Appeal
Courier-Journal & Times
Daily News
Daytona Beach Morning Journal
Ebony Magazine
Entertainment Weekly
Esquire Magazine
Evening Independent
Evening News
Hartford Times
Hattiesburg American
The Hour
The Independent
Jackson Advocate
Jackson Daily News
Jet Magazine
Leisure
Life Magazine
Look Magazine
Los Angeles Times
New York Amsterdam
New York Journal-American
New York Post
New York Times
New York Times Magazine
New York World-Telegram
Newsday
Newsweek

Pittsburgh Courier
People
Saturday Evening Post
Show Business Illustrated
State Times
Sunday Gazette
Time Magazine
Toledo Blade
True: The Man's Magazine
Tuesday Magazine
TV Guide
Variety
Village Voice
Wall Street Journal
World

Records and CDs

Cosby, Bill
    200 M.P.H.
    Bill Cosby Is A Very Funny Fellow, Right!
    I Started Out as a Child
    It's True! It's True!
    Revenge
    To Russell, My Brother, Whom I Slept With
    When I Was a Kid
    Why Is There Air?
    Wonderfulness
Gregory, Dick
    Dick Gregory: The Light Side: The Dark Side
    Dick Gregory On:
    Dick Gregory Talks Turkey
    East and West
    In Living Black & White
    My Brother's Keeper
    Running for President
    The Two Sides of Dick Gregory

Books

Bogle, Donald. *Prime Time Blues: African Americans on Network Television.* New York: Farrar Straus Giroux, 2001.

Cosby, Bill. *Childhood*. New York: G. P. Putnam's Sons, 1991.
Cosby, Bill, and Alvin F. Poussaint. *Come On People!: On the Path from Victims to Victors*. Nashville, TN: Thomas Nelson, 2007.
Dittmer, John. *Local People: The Struggle for Civil Rights in Mississippi*. Champaign: University of Illinois Press, 1995.
Du Bois, W.E.B. *Souls of Black Folk*. New York: Dover Publications, 1994, originally published in 1903.
Foner, Eric. *Give Me Liberty!: An American History*, vol. II, 3rd ed. New York: W.W. Norton & Co., 2012.
Gaines, Kevin. *American Africans in Ghana: Black Expatriates and the Civil Rights Era*. Chapel Hill: University of North Carolina Press, 2008.
Gayle Plummer, Brenda. *In Search of Power: African Americans in the Era of Decolonization, 1956–1974*. New York: Cambridge University Press, 2012.
Goudsouzian, Aram. *Down to the Crossroads: Civil Rights, Black Power, and the Meredith March Against Fear*. New York: Farrar, Straus and Giroux, 2014.
———. *Sidney Poitier: Man, Actor, Icon*. Chapel Hill: University of North Carolina Press, 2003.
Gregory, Dick. *Callus on My Soul: A Memoir*. New York: Kensington Publishing Corp., 2000.
———. *From the Back of the Bus*. New York: Avon Books, 1966.
———. *Nigger: An Autobiography by Dick Gregory*. New York: Pocket Books, 1964.
———. *Write Me In!*. New York: Bantam Books, 1968.
Haggins, Bambi. *Laughing Mad: The Black Comic Persona in Post-Soul America*. New Brunswick, NJ: Rutgers University Press, 2007.
Hill, Lance. *The Deacons for Defense: Armed Resistance and the Civil Rights Movement*. Chapel Hill: University of North Carolina Press, 2004.
Joseph, Peniel. *Waiting 'Til the Midnight Hour: A Narrative History of Black Power in America*. New York: Holt and Co., 2006.
Lane, Mark, and Dick Gregory. *Murder in Memphis: The FBI and the Assassination of Martin Luther King* (originally titled *Code Name Zorro*). New York: Thunder's Mouth Press, 1977.
Lee, Billy, with Dick Lally. *The Wrong Stuff*. New York: Viking, 1984.
Levenstein, Lisa. *A Movement Without Marches: African American Women and the Politics of Poverty in Postwar Philadelphia*. Chapel Hill: The University of North Carolina Press, 2009.
Lipsyte, Robert. *An Accidental Sportswriter: A Memoir*. New York: Harper-Collins, 2011.
Litwack, Leon F. *Trouble in Mind: Black Southerners in the Age of Jim Crow*. New York: Alfred A. Knopf, 1998.
McCluskey, Audrey Thomas, ed. *Richard Pryor: The Life and Legacy of a "Crazy" Black Man*. Bloomington: Indiana University Press.

Meriwether, James. *Proudly We Can Be Africans: Black Americans and Africa, 1935-1961*. Chapel Hill: University of North Carolina Press, 2002.

Miller, Patrick, and David Wiggins, eds. *Sport and the Color Line: Black Athletes and Race Relations in Twentieth Century America*. New York: Routledge, 2003.

Moritz, Charles. *Current Biography Yearbook 1986*. Bronx, NY: H.W. Wilson Co., 1987.

Nachman, Gerald. *Seriously Funny: The Rebel Comedians of the 1950s and 1960s*. New York: Pantheon Books, 2003.

Nkrumah, Kwame. *Ghana: The Autobiography of Kwame Nkrumah*. New York: International Publishers, 1957.

Plummer, Brenda Gayle. *In Search of Power: African Americans in the Era of Decolonization, 1956-1974*. New York: Cambridge University Press, 2012.

Primm, James Neal. *Lion of the Valley: St. Louis, Missouri, 1764-1980*. St. Louis: Missouri Historical Society Press, 1981.

Raymond, Emily. *Stars for Freedom: Hollywood, Black Celebrities, and the Civil Rights Movement*. Seattle: University of Washington Press, 2015.

Smith, Ronald L. *Cosby: The Life of a Comic Legend*. Amherst, NY: Prometheus Books, 1997.

Smith, Suzanne. *Dancing in the Streets: Motown and the Politics of Detroit*. New York: Holt Paperbacks, 2007.

Tygiel, Jules. *Baseball's Great Experiment: Jackie Robinson and His Legacy*. New York: Oxford University Press, 2008.

Van Deburg, William. *New Day in Babylon: The Black Power Movement and American Culture, 1965-1975*. Chicago: University of Chicago Press, 1993.

Ward, Brian. *Just My Soul Responding: Rhythm and Blues, Black Consciousness and Race Relations*. Berkeley: University of California Press, 1998.

Watkins, Mel. *On the Real Side: A History of African American Comedy*. New York: Simon & Schuster, 1994.

Weigley, Russell F., ed. *Philadelphia: A 300-Year History*. New York: W.W. Norton & Co, Inc., 1982.

Wiggins, David. *Glory Bound: Black Athletes in a White America*. Syracuse, NY: Syracuse University Press, 1997.

Articles and Dissertations

Asher, Robert. "Documents of the Race Riot at East Saint Louis." *Journal of the Illinois State Historical Society* 65, no. 3 (Autumn, 1972): 327.

Cosby, Bill. "An Integration of the Visual Media via *Fat Albert and the Cosby Kids* into the Elementary School Curriculum as a Teaching Aid and Vehicle to Achieve Increased Learning." PhD diss., University of Massachusetts, 1976.

Gordon, Dexter B. "Humor in African American Discourse: Speaking of Oppression." *Journal of Black Studies* 29, no. 2 (November 1998): 274.

Harris, Ethel Patricia. "An Afrocentric view of the Rhetoric of Dick Gregory." PhD diss., Ohio State University, 1982.

Minchond, Timothy J., and John A. Salmond. "'The Saddest Story of the Whole Movement': The Clyde Kennard Case and the Search for Racial Reconciliation in Mississippi, 1955–2007." *Journal of Mississippi History* 71, no. 3 (Fall 2009): 193.

Mintz, Lawrence. "Standup Comedy as Social and Cultural Mediation." *American Quarterly* 37, no. 1 (Spring 1985): 71, 78.

Nimako, Kwame. "Nkrumah, African Awakening and Neo-colonialism: How Black America Awakened Nkrumah and Nkrumah Awakened Black America." *The Black Scholar* 40, no. 2 (Summer 2010): 55.

Oliar, Dotan, and Christopher Sprigman, "There's No Free Laugh (Anymore): The Emergence of Intellectual Property Norms and the Transformation of Stand-Up Comedy." *Virginia Law Review* 94, no. 8 (December 2008): 1793.

Whitman, Arthur. "Bill Cosby: The Spy Who Knocked 'Em Cold." *True: The Man's Magazine* 48, no. 356 (January 1967): 80.

Index

A&T University. *See* student sit-ins (1960)
ACT!, 55
Africa: politics. *See* Ghana
African American images on television, 64–65
African American music: crossover sales, 36
Alabama church bombing (1963), 53, 73
Ali, Muhammad, xv, 41, 46, 81, 83, 101, 105, 113–114, 116
American Guild of Variety Artists (AGVA), 26, 28
Associated Press, 55–56
Atlanta restaurant protests (1964), 53–54

Baldwin, James, 52, 100
Barnett, Ross (Governor), 43–44, 49, 51
Belafonte, Harry, xv, xvii, 41, 46, 48, 58, 63, 83
Bell, Aubrey, 42–43
Berry, Faith, xx, 104, 105
Bilbo, Theodore (Senator), 43
Bill Cosby Is a Very Funny Fellow, Right! (album), 22, 57
Bill Cosby on Prejudice (TV special), 108–110

The Bill Cosby Show (TV series), 102, 103–104
Black History: Lost, Stolen or Strayed (TV documentary), 86–87
Black Power movement, xviii, xix, 67, 70, 71, 74–76, 78, 79, 82, 86, 101
blaxploitation film cycle, 107–108
Bogle, Donald, 64
Brown, James, 76
Brown, Luvaghn, 45
Brown v. Board of Education of Topeka, Kansas, xviii, 37, 71, 125–126
Bruce, Lenny, 28, 33, 118
Bunche, Ralph, 21, 48, 94
Bush, George W. (President), 125

Calhoun, Lillian, 62
Callus On My Soul (book), 118
Cambridge, Godfrey, 83, 100
Campbell, Bruce, 102
Campbell, Silver and Cosby Corporation (CS&C), 81, 102
Carmichael, Stokely, 69, 71, 72, 73, 74, 75, 78, 81, 85, 86, 105
Carroll, Diahann, 102
Carson, Johnny, 58, 60. *See also Tonight Show*
Chicago Defender, 24–25, 46, 49, 51, 56, 57

Chicago Society of Writers and Editors, 100
Childhood (book), 2
Civil Rights Act of 1964, 71
Civil Rights Movement, xvii, xviii, xx, xxi, 15, 16, 19, 36, 37, 38, 41, 42, 43, 58, 63, 67, 71, 76–77, 85, 89, 96, 100, 129. See also Mississippi racism and politics
Clay, Cassius, 81. See also Ali, Muhammad
Coates, Ta-Nehisi, 123, 126
Coleman, James, 76, 77
Colpix Records, 21, 37
Come On, People!: On the Path from Victims to Victors (book), 127
Conference of Nonaligned Third World Nations, 94. See also Gregory, Dick: Africa visits by
Congress of Racial Equality (CORE), 56, 72
Correction Connection. See Gregory, Dick: business enterprises of
Cosby (TV series), 124
Cosby, Anna, 4, 10, 11, 12
Cosby, Bill, xv, xvi, xvii, xviii, xx, xxi, 57, (pl. D), (pl. F), 110–111, 119, 122; African American criticism of, 85, 126; anti-Dick Gregory persona of, xix, 34, 35, 42, 57, 70–71, 74, 81; athletic achievements of, 18–19, 32, (pl. B); awards received by, 22, 65, 125; on Black Power movement, 70; childhood of, 2–3, 4, 7–10, 12, 16, 105; criticisms of, xx; and criticisms of celebrity activists, 81; cultural activism of, 85–86, 87–88, 124; on death of son Ennis, 125; deracialized humor, of, xix, xx, 12, 22, 34–35, 36, 57–58, 60, 62–63, 83, 84; deracialized image of, 83–84, 85, 86, 101, 103, 104, 105; desexualized persona of, 58–59; early career of, 31–36, 37, 42; education of, xx, 16–17, 18, 90, 106–107, 128; on *The Electric Company*, 107; experiences of racism by, 18; and *Fat Albert and His Friends* (TV series), 106; and *Fat Albert and the Cosby Kids* (TV series), 107; on Dick Gregory, 119, 120; Dick Gregory views of, 96–97; on Hollywood racial subjects, 65, 81–82, 85–86, 87; on Hollywood racial stereotyping, 123; incarceration of, xx 128; income and wealth of, xx, 42, 66, 71, 81, 122; and Jemmin, Inc., 102–103; Navy service of, 17–18; "Neanderthal" routine of, 60–62; and "A Nut in Every Car routine, 57; philanthropic activities of, 123; and "The Playground" (1966), 8–9; and political avoidance, 74, 101; and political participation, 63, 71, 78, 122; and "Pound Cake Speech" (2004), xx, 125–126, 127, 128; production company of, 102–103; on protest politics, 66; racial humor of, 33; racial politics of, 70, 81; and sanitizing of background in comedy routines, 11, 17, 62, 128; and "selling out" controversies, 83; on *Sesame Street*, 107; sexual allegations against, xx, 127–129; success of, 89–90, 102, 120. See also *The Cosby Show*, *I Spy*
Cosby, Camille (Hanks), 41, 62
Cosby, Ennis: murder of, 124
The Cosby Show, xx, 120–123, 128
Crosson, Lesley, 99–100
Culp, Robert, 63, 65, 82, 84, 86

Daley, Richard (Mayor), 79, 90–91, 93

Index

Dancing in the Street: Motown and the Cultural Politics of Detroit (book), xvii
Davis, Ossie, xvii, 56, 59, 63, (pl. E), 95, 100
Davis, Jr., Sammy, xv, xvii, 28, 48, 59, 76, 77, 85, 102
Dee, Ruby, xvii, 100
Dick Gregory Health Enterprises, 113
Dick Gregory: The Light Side: The Dark Side (album), 90–92
Dick Gregory's Natural Diet for Folks Who Eat: Cookin' with Mother Nature (book), 99
Dick Gregory's Slim-Safe Bahamian Diet, 115
Dittmer, John, 43, 45, 47, 51
Dobbs Houses, Inc., 53–54
Douglas, Mike, (pl. C)
Dreir, Alex, 21
Du Bois, W.E.B., xviii, 81, 94, 129, 144n67
Duckett, Al, 100
Dunham, Katherine, 117
Dyson, Michael Eric, 126

Ebony, 58–59, 98
Esterow, Milton, 51, 52
Evers, Charles, 75, 77, 78
Evers, Medgar, 47, 72, 118

Fair Employment Practices Commission, 71
Farrakhan, Louis, 119
Foner, Eric, 54
Formula Four X, xx, 100, 114. *See also* Gregory, Dick: health activism
Foxx, Redd, xvi, 38–39

Gart, Herb, 32
Garvey, Marcus, 86, 93, 94
Gaslight Café, 32–33, 36
Ghana, 93–94
Give Us the Children (documentary), 105–106
Gordon, Dexter, xv–xvi, 29
Goudsouzian, Aram, xvii, 74
Gregory, Christian, 119, 120
Gregory, Dick, xv, xvi, xvii, xviii, xix, xx, xxi, 21, 33, 64, 67, (pl. A), (pl. C), 81, 83, 86, 105, 108, 110–111, 129; and ABC News documentary (1961), 28; Africa visits by, 94, 95, 114; African American criticism of, 39, 48, 80, 81; anti-drug views of, 99, 117; anti-poverty activism of, 100–101; antiestablishment views of, 92; and Apex Club, 24–25, 26; athletic background of, 12–14, 16, 18; and Australian government, 95; awards given to, 38; on Black Power movement, 70, 78; business enterprises of, 115–116; and capitalism, 79, 92, 116; celebrity athlete endorsements for, 114; and Central Intelligence Agency (CIA), 95; childhood of, 1–2, 3, 5–7, 10–11, 12–15; college appearances by, 90–92, 97–98; as college dropout, 16, 19; commodification of African American humor by, 39–40; college education of, 50; congressional appearance of, 38; on Bill Cosby, 96–97; death of, 119; early career of, 22–31; and experiences of racism, 28, 38; FBI file of, 118; and health activism, 99, 100–101, 113–116; and Food for Freedom Drive, 45–47, 49; Hollywood fears of, 57, 64; and human rights work, xx, 96, 97, 98; and comparisons to Bill Cosby, 10, 34, 104; imprisonment of, 74, 99; income and expenses of, xx, 36,

Gregory, Dick *(continued)*
37, 38, 41, 52, 74, 77, 79, 98, 116; interaction with white audience members, 38, 39; on liberalism, 44; and March on Washington (1963), 53; mail-order businesses of, 115; mayoral campaign of, 79; media silence on death of, 119–120; and the Meredith March (1966), 71–74, 78, 85; on *The Mike Douglas Show*, (pl. C); Mississippi attacks on, 47, 48, 49; and Mississippi food drive, 44–47; military service of, 17, 23; and Native American rights, 96, 99; and nightclub prejudicial practices, 98–99; political activism of, xix, 14–16, 38, 41, 42, 43–44, 47–57, 59, 63, 66, (pl. E), 69, 72–74, 76, 77, 79, 89–93, 95–99, 100, 101, 117; political content in comedy of, 23, 27, 37, 51, 117; presidential campaign of, 79–80, 98; and Queens Club controversy, 52–53; racial content in comedy of, 21, 22, 29–31, 36, 37, 51–52, 58, 79–80; on religion, 44; and Herman Roberts nightclub, 26, 28; shooting of, 55, 76; and show business career conversion and decline, 79, 96, 100, 117, 118, 119; and sit-ins, 15, 37, 53, 54; at Southern Illinois University (SIU), 14, 16, 23, 24, (pl. A); threats against, 82, 118; and Tougaloo College event, (1966), 76, 77; as trailblazer, 23, 38–39. *See also* Civil Rights Movement
Gregory, Lillian, 26, 54, 73, 91, 94
Gregory, Lucille, 3, 5, 13
Griffin, John Howard, 50–51
Guess Who's Coming to Dinner (film), 86

Hefner, Hugh M., xviii, 29, 37
Hepburn, Dave, 30, 36, 52, 57, 65
Hicks, James, 66–67
Hill, Lance, 42
Hoover, J. Edgar, 118
Hope, Bob, 26, 27, 37
Hudson, Walter, 113, 115

I Spy (TV series), xix, 63–64, 65, 66, 78, 81, 82, 84, 86, 87, 103, 104, 124. *See also* Cosby, Bill
I Started Out as a Child (album), 60
In Living Black & White (album), 21–22, 37

The Jack Paar Show, xix, 21, 37, 38
Jackson, Jesse, 91, 100
Jet magazine, 94, 102, 113
Jim Crow and segregation, xvii, xxi, 15, 22, 30, 31, 37, 39, 46, 49, 53, 55, 59, 63, 77, 81, 129
Johnson, Bob, 113
Johnson, Lyndon B., 22
Julia (TV series), 102

Karnow, Stanley, 63
Kennard, Clyde, 49, 50–51
Kennedy, John F. (President), 37, 49, 69, 95, 118
Key, Keegan-Michael, 126–127
Key & Peele (TV series), 126–127
King, Martin Luther Jr., xviii, 46, 48, 69, 71, 72, 73, 74, 76, 77, 81, 85, 90, 94, 95, 97, 101, 105, 114, 116, 118, 124
Korean War, 13, 17

Lee, Bill "Spaceman," 114
Leonard, Sheldon, 63
Let's Do It Again (film), (pl. F), 108
Lewis, John (SNCC chairman), 54, 75–76, 81

Local People: The Struggle for Civil Rights in Mississippi (book), 43
Lord Buckley, 33
Lynch, Philip, 95
Lynn, Conrad, 80

Mabley, Moms, 38
Malcolm X, xviii, 55, 56, 65, 81, 85, 95, 97, 105, 118, 119, 129
Man and Boy (film), 107
Mann, Ralph, 79
March Against Fear (1966). *See* Gregory, Dick: Meredith March
Mason, Benjamin and Pearl, 8
Mathis, Greg, 126
McCain, W.D., 50
McKissick, Floyd, 72, 73, 78
Meredith, James, 49–50, 71–72, 73, 74, 75, 76, 77
Meredith, Lee (sheriff), 72
Miller, Marvin, 107
Millstein, Gilbert, 37–38
Mintz, Lawrence, xvi, 17
Mississippi racism and politics, 42–44, 45, 47–50, 69, 71–72, 76. *See also* Civil Rights Movement; Gregory, Dick: Food for Freedom Drive
Monroe, Al, 39
Moynihan Report (1965). See *The Negro Family: The Case for National Action*
Murphy, Eddie, 118, 120
My Brother's Keeper (album), 42, 43–44, 45

National Association for the Advancement of Colored People (NAACP), 44, 45, 47, 49, 63, 72, 81, 125
National Broadcasting Company (NBC), 66, 83, 84, 102, 105, 106, 121, 123–124

National Coalition against War, Racism and Repression, (pl. E)
National Urban League, 74, 80
The Negro Family: The Case for National Action (The Moynihan Report), 87
The New Bill Cosby Show (TV series), 106
the New Deal, 8
New York Amsterdam News, 30, 36, 44, 95, 99–100, 124
New York Post, 52, 79
the New York Society for Ethical Culture, 64
New York Times, 22, 32–33, 51, 92, 96, 99, 104, 106, 118, 120
Newsday, 84
Newsweek magazine, 30, 57, 81, 83–84, 97, 99
Nigger (book), 1, 56, 73
Nimako, Kwame, 93
Nkrumah, Kwame, 93–94

Paar, Jack, 39, 58. See also *Jack Paar Show*
Patterson, Lindsay, 92–93
Pearson, Drew, 79
Peele, Jordan, 126–127
Philadelphia: and African-American migration, 11; African-American education in, 16–17
The Philosophy and Opinions of Marcus Garvey (book), 93
A Piece of the Action (film), 108
Pinckney, Darryl, 120, 121
Pitts, Jr., Leonard, 126
Playboy magazine, 29
the Playboy Club (Chicago), 29, 30, 31, 37, 38, 40
Poitier, Sidney, xvii, xviii, 48, 58, (pl. F), 86, 104, 108
Poussaint, Alvin, 127

Powell, Jr., Adam Clayton, 78, 94
Prime Time Blues: African Americans on Network Television (book), 64
Pryor, Richard, 23, 82–83, 118, 120
Pugh, Douglas, 64

racism and racial stereotyping in early African American comedy, 26–27
Rashad, Phylicia, 120
Raymond, Emily, xvii
Richardson, Gloria, 55
Robinson, Jackie, xvii, xviii, 22, 46, 48, 67, 120, 129
Rogers, Timmie, xvi, 27, 38
Ross, Fred, 46–47
Russell, Nipsey, xvi, 27, 28, 33, 38, 39

SCLC. *See* Southern Christian Leadership Conference
SNCC. *See* Student Nonviolent Coordinating Committee
Sahl, Mort, 27–28, 33
The Sammy Davis, Jr. Show (TV series), 102. *See also* Davis, Jr., Sammy
The Second Bill Cosby Special (TV), (pl. D)
See, Hilda, 36
Sherman, Allan, 22
Show Business Illustrated, 38
Sidney Poitier: Man, Actor, Icon (book), xvii
Silver, Roy, 34, 35, 71, 102, 103
Smith, Don, 56
Smith, Ronald, 59, 62, 104, 120, 124–125
Smith, Suzanne, xvii
Souls of Black Folk (book), 144n67
Southern Christian Leadership Conference (SCLC), 76
St. Louis, MO racial history, 4, 5, 12, 15–16

Stargell, Willie, 114
Stars for Freedom: Hollywood, Black Celebrities, and the Civil Rights Movement (book), xvii
Student Nonviolent Coordinating Committee, 45, 53, 54, 55, 75

Till, Emmett, 47. *See also* Mississippi racism and politics
To All My Friends On Shore (TV movie), 107
To Russell, My Brother, Whom I Slept With (album), 84–85
The Tonight Show, xix, 60
Ture, Kwame. *See* Carmichael, Stokely
Tygiel, Jules, xvii

Uptown Saturday Night (film), 108

Van Landingham, Zack, 50
Vietnam war, xix, 48, 69, 89, 95, 99
Voting Rights Act of, 1965, 43, 71

Walker, Jesse H., 39, 59–60, 64
Walsh, Maximilian, 95
Ward, Brian, 36
Washington, Harold (Mayor), 79
Watkins, Jr., Joseph, 56
Watts riots (1965), 55–56
Wechsler, James, 52
Wells, Rolla (Mayor), 4
White, Slappy, 27, 38
Why Is There Air? (album), 67
Williams, Bert, xvi
Williams, Richard M., 96
Wilson, Flip, xvi, 83
World War I, 11
World War II, 11, 43
Wright, Richard, 94
Write Me In! (book), 79–80, 98

Young, Whitney, 74, 80

www.ingramcontent.com/pod-product-compliance
Ingram Content Group UK Ltd.
Pitfield, Milton Keynes, MK11 3LW, UK
UKHW011519100725
460636UK00015B/222